The Critical Idiom

General Editor: JOHN D. JUMP

7 Satire

Satire / *Arthur Pollard*

Methuen & Co Ltd

First published 1970
by Methuen & Co Ltd,
11 New Fetter Lane, London EC4
© 1970 Arthur Pollard
Printed in Great Britain
by Cox & Wyman Ltd, Fakenham, Norfolk

SBN 416 17230 X Hardback
SBN 416 17240 7 Paperback

Distributed in the U.S.A.
by Barnes & Noble Inc.

for BONAMY DOBRÉE
most inspiring of teachers

Contents

General Editor's Preface

This volume is one of a series of short studies, each dealing with a single key item, or a group of two or three key items, in our critical vocabulary. The purpose of the series differs from that served by the standard glossaries of literary terms. Many terms are adequately defined for the needs of students by the brief entries in these glossaries, and such terms will not be the subjects of studies in the present series. But there are other terms which cannot be made familiar by means of compact definitions. Students need to grow accustomed to them through simple and straightforward but reasonably full discussions of them. The purpose of this series is to provide such discussions.

Some of the terms in question refer to literary movements (e.g., 'Romanticism', 'Aestheticism', etc.), others to literary kinds (e.g., 'Comedy', 'Epic', etc.), and still others to stylistic features (e.g., 'Irony', 'The Conceit', etc.). Because of this diversity of subject-matter, no attempt has been made to impose a uniform pattern upon the studies. But all authors have tried to provide as full illustrative quotation as possible, to make reference whenever appropriate to more than one literature, and to compose their studies in such a way as to guide readers towards the short bibliographies in which they have made suggestions for further reading.

John D. Jump

University of Manchester

The proper study of Mankind is Man ...
Sole judge of Truth, in endless Error hurl'd:
The glory, jest and riddle of the world.
(Pope, *Essay on Man* II. 2, 17–18)

Tremble and turn pale
When Satire wields her mighty flail.
(Charles Churchill, *The Ghost*, III. 925–6)

I

Aims and Attitudes

The satirist is not an easy man to live with. He is more than usually conscious of the follies and vices of his fellows and he cannot stop himself from showing that he is. He is in a difficult position, for he can so easily lay himself open to the charge of moral superiority or even of hypocrisy if people think that they see in him the faults he condemns in others. If he escape these charges, he may still have to counter that of mere personal animosity against his victims, of being 'a mean spiteful little wretch', as Humbert Wolfe described Pope (*Notes on English Verse Satire*, 1929, p. 105). Like the preacher, the satirist seeks to persuade and convince, but his position in relation to those he addresses is more delicate and more difficult than that of the preacher. The latter seeks primarily to make his hearers accept virtue; the former must make his readers agree with him in identifying and condemning behaviour and men he regards as vicious. These men are our fellow-beings, and the vast majority of us would prefer not to condemn, if only because we recognize that 'There but for the grace of God go I'. The satirist may seem to condemn too easily, even to enjoy doing it. His enthusiasm with verbal bludgeon, rapier or 'mighty flail' is often the evidence of such enjoyment. He asks us to admire the skill with which he uses these weapons, to recognize him as an artist and satire as an art.

This desire, however, is usually implicit. Though he may enjoy his talent and may hope that we will enjoy it too, the satirist normally avows a more serious intent. Dr Johnson in the *Dictionary* defined satire as 'a poem in which wickedness or folly is censured'. Dryden and Defoe went further than this, the one in claiming that 'the true end of satire is the amendment of vices' (*Discourse Concerning Satire*), the other that 'the end of Satyr is Reformation: and the Author, tho' he doubts the work of Conversion is at a general Stop, has put his Hand to the Plow' (Preface to *The True Born Englishman*).[1] They both believe that satire can heal and restore, even though Defoe is rather doubtful of his own contemporaries. With his characteristic pessimism Swift had fewer doubts. In the preface to *The Battle of the Books* (1704) he wrote:

> Satire is a sort of glass, wherein beholders do generally discover everybody's face but their own, which is the chief reason for that kind of reception it meets in the world, and that so very few are offended with it.

and at a later date (1728) he saw satire as at best a kind of moral policeman restraining the righteous but helpless against the wicked, assisting 'to preserve well inclin'd men in the course of virtue but seldom or never reclaim[ing] the vicious'. Satire as healer and corrective gives way to satire as punishment. In that great and gloomy work *The Epilogue to the Satires* (1738), as the ageing and crippled poet drew to the end of what he called that 'long disease, [his] life', Pope looked around, believing that, like the Hebrew prophets of old, he stood alone to denounce what was beyond redeeming (Dialogue I. 141–70):

> Yes, I am proud; I must be proud to see
> Men not afraid of God, afraid of me:
> Safe from the Bar, the Pulpit, and the Throne,
> Yet touch'd and sham'd by *Ridicule* alone.
>   O sacred Weapon! left for Truth's defence,
> Sole Dread of Folly, Vice, and Insolence!
> To all but Heav'n-directed hands deny'd,
> The Muse may give thee, but the Gods must guide.
> Rev'rent I touch thee!
>
> (Dialogue II. 208–16)

[1] I am grateful to my colleague Mr A. W. Bower of the University of Hull for drawing my attention to this quotation and to that from *The Intelligencer* on p. 73.

The reference to 'Truth's defence' reminds us of the satirist as guardian of ideals. The best satire, that which is surest in tone, is that which is surest in its values. In our own literature the age of Pope and of all those quoted in the previous paragraph provided our best satire – because in that Augustan age (the epithet itself a mark of confidence in its achievement and attainment) men felt sure of the standards to which they could refer. Indeed, much both of the sorrow and the anger in Pope's last works derives from the feeling that those standards had collapsed:

> Truth, Worth, Wisdom daily they decry –
> 'Nothing is Sacred now but Villany.'
>
> (Dialogue I. 169–70)

Satire is always acutely conscious of the difference between what things are and what they ought to be. The satirist is often a minority figure; he cannot, however, afford to be a declared outcast. For him to be successful his society should at least pay lip-service to the ideals he upholds. If it does, he is placed in a more subtle and potentially more effective position than that of simple denouncer of vice. He is then able to exploit more fully the differences between appearance and reality and especially to expose hypocrisy. The hypocrite's skin is notoriously more tender than that of the openly vicious. The one has nothing to conceal, the other everything. His whole reputation is at stake. Openly he subscribes to the ideals that secretly he ignores or defies.

Such a man, we may feel, deserves exposure. To this extent the satirist is performing a socially and morally useful task of universal validity. Dr Johnson, however, would distinguish between general and particular satire: 'Proper *Satire* is distinguished, by the generality of the reflections, from a lampoon which is aimed at a particular person' (*Dictionary*). Pope had other views:

> F. Spare then the Person, and expose the Vice,
> P. How Sir! not damn the Sharper, but the Dice?
>
> (*Epilogue to the Satires*, Dialogue II. 12–13)

But the lampoon can have a more than personal application. When Pope attacks Atticus or Sporus in the *Epistle to Dr Arbuthnot*, he is attacking not only Addison and Hervey but all those who resemble what he claims they are, all who are accomplished but aloof, jealous and complacent, all superficial, effeminate, flattering, scandal-mongering persons. Nevertheless, there are dangers in personal satire. No matter how much its point and penetration in its own day, in time it may easily lose its point. Its sheer topicality may obscure or obliterate its universality. Thus many of the Grub-Street writers in *The Dunciad* and their fellows in Dryden's *MacFlecknoe* are now mere names, and even when the industry of scholars has rescued the contemporary relevance of a reference, it may still remain remote and lacking in any immediate relevance to us. In this context, however, we need to remember that the act of writing badly is not for us so great a crime as it was for Pope and his contemporaries. The satirist needs to know what he can convince his audience of as being important. If he gives too much rein to his own hobby-horse, as Juvenal does in his misogynistic sixth Satire, reaching a crescendo with the accusation that women had become so depraved that they had even taken to learning Greek, he is likely to find that his audience is laughing at him instead of at his intended victims.

The satirist has to be careful, but in one respect he has extensive freedom. He does not labour under any formal restraint, for the variety of satire is almost infinite. This variety has never been better summarized than by A. Melville Clark, who, confining himself to what he calls regular verse satire, says:

> It swings backwards and forwards, on an ellipse about the two foci of the satiric universe, the exposure of folly and the castigation of vice; it fluctuates between the flippant and the earnest, the completely trivial and the heavily didactic; it ranges from extremes of crudity and brutality to the utmost refinement and elegance; it employs singly or in conjunction monologue, dialogue, epistle, oration, narrative,

manners-painting, character-drawing, allegory, fantasy, travesty, burlesque, parody, and any other vehicle it chooses; and it presents a chameleon-like surface by using all the tones of the satiric spectrum, wit, ridicule, irony, sarcasm, cynicism, the sardonic and invective.

(*Studies in Literary Modes,* 1946, p. 32)

We should, however, make some immediate distinctions, distinctions respectively between the satiric and comic and the satiric and ironic. Irony is in Clark's list as a tone of satire, and there is satiric irony. There is also satiric comedy – just another reminder that satire is not in itself a pure and exclusive form. But there are also comedy and irony that are not satiric, comedy that is more generous and irony that is more serious than satire. Such comedy is kindly; it makes fun but accepts, it criticizes but appreciates; it laughs at but also laughs with its butt. Such is the comedy of Shakespeare's Falstaff. Irony more serious than satire knows no bounds short of melancholia and madness. Its seriousness loses perspective; it is marked by ferocity and gloom. Such is the irony of Swift's *Modest Proposal* to cure the poverty and over-population of Ireland by the systematic rearing of its children as meat for the tables of the wealthy. Such is Hardy's fierce indictment of ironic disposition after the execution of Tess, the 'pure woman': 'Justice was done. The President of the Immortals had finished his sport with Tess', or his cryptic celebration of 'Christmas: 1924':

> 'Peace upon earth!' was said. We sing it,
> And pay a million priests to bring it.
> After two thousand years of mass
> We've got as far as poison gas.

2

Subjects

Whatever be these exclusions, it is a wide range which covers both 'the flippant and the earnest', especially when we note that these are mixed with other contradictions to make man 'the glory, jest and riddle of the world' (Pope, *Essay on Man* II. 18). Juvenal knew how much was his:

> quidquid agunt homines, votum timor ira voluptas
> gaudia discursus, nostri farrago libelli est.
>
> (*Satires* I. 85–6)
>
> (Whatever men do – vow, fear, anger, pleasure, joys, employments – is the motley subject of our little book.)

Whatever men do, or perhaps better, remembering the satirist's critical eye, whatever they 'get up to'. In Juvenal's case this covers in various satires the conditions of life in Rome (III), the behaviour of Domitian to his cabinet council (IV), the character of women (VI) and the 'vanity of human wishes' (X), whilst a single satire may be, as Nettleship observed of the first, 'a series of incoherent complaints ... A married impotent, an athletic lady, a barber rich enough to challenge the fortunes of all the patricians: the Egyptian Crispinus with his ring, the lawyer Matho in his litter: the infamous will-hunter, the robber of his ward, the plunderer of the provinces: the pander husband, the low-born spendthrift, the forger, the poisoner; all these are hurried together in no intelligible order' (*Journal of Philology* XVI (1888), pp. 62–3). Only Pope can rival Juvenal in the all-embracing character of his satire, but Pope focuses more precisely on his object or, rather, he keeps his audience more insistently in mind of it. 'Satire,' says

Ian Jack, 'is born of the instinct to protest; it is protest become art' (*Pope*, 1954 (Writers and Their Work), p. 17). The satirist looks around him and cannot help himself:

> quem patitur dormire nurus corruptor avarae
> quem sponsae turpes et praetextatus adulter?
>
> (Juvenal, *Satires* I. 77–8)

(Whom does the corruptor of a covetous daughter-in-law allow to sleep? whom base brides and the teenage adulterer?)

But the subject must be worthwhile. Juvenal felt that his age was so bad that it was difficult *not* to write satire (ibid., I. 30). At times, however, he seems to be too troubled over too little. Those are the occasions when we wonder whether protest has become art. The 'spontaneous overflow of powerful feelings' has not been subjected to the discipline of art. Here again a contrast with Pope is helpful, for whereas he destroys his victims by a relentless and penetrating finesse, Juvenal too often thrashes blindly around with Churchill's 'mighty flail'.

The subject of protest must be worthwhile. It should encompass one or more of the central areas of man's experience. Satire is, however, essentially a social mode; it has nothing in it of the transcendental. It has nothing of 'the world forgetting, by the world forgot'. The experiences which can produce this condition, the experiences, for example, of love and death are in their essential magnificence beyond the reach of satire. In comedy or tragedy they may be celebrated and exalted. Satire does not exalt; it deflates. When therefore it regards these experiences, it is from its own obliquely critical angle and through its own distorting mirror. It can take death and use it to reflect on the life it has closed, perhaps as a reminder of the way a man has been treated and a criticism of those who have treated him thus, as Bufo (Halifax) did Dryden:

> *Dryden* alone escap'd his judging eye:
> But still the Great have kindness in reserve,
> He help'd to bury whom he help'd to starve.
>
> > (Pope, *Epistle to Dr Arbuthnot*, 246–8)

or as a comment on the way a man himself has lived, as in Byron's description of George III, ineffectual king in an age of tyranny:

> In the first year of freedom's second dawn
> > Died George the Third: although no tyrant, one
> Who shielded tyrants, till each sense withdrawn
> > Left him nor mental nor external sun: ...
>
> He died! his death made no great stir on earth:
> > His burial made some pomp; there was profusion
> Of velvet, gilding, brass, and no great dearth
> > Of aught but tears – save those shed by collusion....
>
> It seem'd the mockery of hell to fold
> The rottenness of eighty years in gold.
>
> > (*The Vision of Judgment*, 57–60, 65–8, 79–80)

Even here, however, Byron is concerned not so much with George III's death as with his funeral. There is another reference – to the death of Louis XVI by the guillotine. It occurs on the arrival of George at heaven's gate and St Peter is speaking:

> 'Well! he won't find kings to jostle
> Him on his way; but does he wear his head?
> > Because the last we saw here had a tustle,
> And ne'er would have got into heaven's good graces,
> Had he not flung his head in all our faces.
>
> > (Ibid., 140–4)

This shows us how careful the satirist must be. There are too many unpleasant associations here for this to be wholly successful – except in developing still further the impression of St Peter's cantankerous nature. We cannot joke about the deaths of others; we can about our own. But few have been courageous enough to do it. Pope was one, when he turned upon his flatterers:

> There are, who to my person pay their court,
> I cough like *Horace*, and tho' lean, am short, ...
> Go on, obliging Creatures, make me see
> All that disgrac'd my Betters, met in me: ...
> And when I die, be sure you let me know
> Great *Homer* dy'd three thousand years ago.
> > (*Epistle to Dr Arbuthnot*, 115–16, 119–20, 123–4)

Swift, at greater length, was another in his *Verses on the Death of Dr Swift*, but his death is the occasion only; the real subject is the reception of the news of his death:

> Behold the fatal Day arrive!
> 'How is the Dean?' 'He's just alive'.
> Now the departing Prayer is read:
> 'He hardly breathes. The Dean is dead.'
>
> > (147–50)

We do not get very near to the dean himself, his feelings or his sufferings; these are not subjects for satire:

> Before the Passing-Bell begun,
> 'The News thro' half the Town is run.
> 'O, may we all for Death prepare!
> What has he left? and who's his Heir?' ...
>
> My female Friends, whose tender Hearts
> Have better learn'd to act their Parts,
> Receive the News in *doleful Dumps*,
> 'The Dean is dead (*and what is Trumps?*)
> 'Then Lord have Mercy on his Soul.
> '(Ladies I'll venture for the *Vole*.)'
>
> > (151–4, 225–30)

Swift is, in fact, using the solemnity of death to criticize the superficialities of the living. This solemnity is equally useful in contexts less obviously superficial. Johnson's *Vanity of Human Wishes* shows, in Gray's phrase, that

> The paths of glory lead but to the grave.

Johnson's is moral satire as in example after example he shows the futility of human ambition. Wolsey's 'last sighs reproach the faith of kings'; 'Hear [Laud's] death, ye blockheads, hear and sleep'; Charles XII's

> fall was destined to a barren strand,
> A petty fortress, and a dubious hand,

(118, 172, 217–18)

and so on.

But after death, what? Johnson ends his poem by counselling (to use his character Nekayah's phrase in *Rasselas*) not a choice of life but of eternity. Religion in its essence, like death, at least in times before our own, was rarely the subject of satire. Men did not criticize God, whatever they did to His so-called followers. And yet satire is one of the means of relief necessary for us to go on facing problems of the highest import. What can be done in employing satire either directly on or indirectly associated with serious subjects will depend to some extent on the relationship of an author to his audience. An author may wish to outrage his audience, to ridicule, in fact, their seriousness. This is undoubtedly an element in Byron's *The Vision of Judgment*. He may wish to expose a hollow seriousness, as with Samuel Butler's *The Way of All Flesh*; or, as in the ages of faith he could do so easily, he may wish to inject some fun alongside, but without challenging, the seriousness. Such is one constituent in the treatment of Noah's stubborn wife in the mystery plays, whilst both fun and satire enter into Boccaccio's story of the immoral monk discovered by his abbot. By a stratagem the monk gives the abbot, as the latter thinks, safe access to the girl. The monk returns and eavesdrops on the abbot. In due course, the abbot not realizing what has happened, the monk is called for punishment. The monk answers:

Messere, io non sono ancora tanto all' ordine di san Benedetto stato, che io possa avere ogni particularità di quello apparata; e voi ancora non m'avavate mostrato ch'e' monaci si debbon far dalle femine premere, come da' digiuni e dalle vigilie; ma ora che mostrato me l'avete, vi prometto, se questa mi perdonate, di mai più in ciò non peccare, anzi farò sempre come io a voi ho veduto fare. – ... e impostogli di ciò che veduto aveva silenzio, onestamente misero la giovinetta di fuori, e poi più volte si dee credere ve la facesser tornare.

(Sir, I have not been so long in the Benedictine Order as to be able to have learnt all its details and you still had not shown me that monks have to burden themselves with women as they do with fasting and with vigils. But now that you have given me a demonstration I promise you that if you excuse this lapse I shall never sin in this respect again; on the contrary I shall always do as I have seen you doing. – ... and swearing him to silence about what he had seen, they let the young girl out with no harm to her reputation, and one must believe that often afterwards they brought her back again.)[1]

(*Decameron*, 1st Day, Novella 4)

There is much that we think of as Chaucerian here. First, there is the straight-faced telling of the story, the skilful play on the reader's anticipation, the neatly turned *dénouement* and, finally, the brief wry comment from the author himself.

Dryden's *Absalom and Achitophel* comes from the very different religious environment of seventeenth-century England with its Puritan controversies. It attacks the ultra-solemn, puritanical, Protestant, bible-centred opponents of the King. They must have been disgusted by what they would consider the poet's licentious use of Scripture. To the King's party, however, this would appear beautifully apt, not least when Dryden used it most daringly and against that most rigid and most gloomy of Puritans, Shimei:

> When two or three were gathered to declaim
> Against the monarch of Jerusalem,
> Shimei was always in the midst of them.

(601–3)

[1] Mr J. R. Woodhouse of the Department of Italian, University of Hull, has kindly supplied this translation.

Such lines with their recollections of our Lord's promise to his followers (Matthew xviii. 20) are well nigh blasphemous, but they fit in Dryden's overall exploitation of biblical allegory. He works rather on the periphery than at the centre. His main reference is to the Old Testament rather than the New, to history rather than revelation, and to a somewhat minor incident at that. In other words, he knew how far he could go to outrage the Puritans thoroughly without outraging his other contemporaries at all. This is the essence of successful satire – to get your victims 'hopping mad' and your audience 'laughing their heads off'.

Faced with the serious demands that religion imposes on man, the satirist delights to make much of the discrepancy between profession and practice. Affectation and hypocrisy are ready topics for him at any time; they take on additional point when those who are guilty of such faults are committed by profession to a very different standard of behaviour. That is why the clergy and all who set themselves up as holy have been perennial subjects for the satirist's attention. They act at once as apology for the *homme moyen sensuel* (they are his scapegoat) and as an opportunity for him to insist first on 'Physician, heal thyself'. Thus we have Burns's unrestrained delight as he exposes the supplicant in 'Holy Willie's Prayer', a petition mingled of secret candour, blind failure to recognize his sinfulness even though he confesses it, an unctuous sense of his own election and a vengeful desire against all who have crossed him. The wit derives from the simplicity, even the stupidity of a confession that does not recognize its own hypocrisy. There is a variant of this in Jonson's *The Alchemist* when Subtle catalogues all the canting practices of the Puritans, whose representatives dare not cross him because they hope by him to be made wealthy, but for a sustained and unrelenting sardonic exposure of religious hypocrisy Molière's *Tartuffe* is unsurpassed. On the one hand, we have the reiterated hostility of Cleanthes and other characters against

> Ces gens qui, par une âme à l'intérêt soumise,
> Font de dévotion métier et marchandise,
> Et veulent acheter crédit et dignités
> A prix de faux clins d'yeux et d'élans affectés.

(those slaves of interest, who make a trade of godliness, and who would purchase honours and reputation with a hypocritical turning up of the eyes and affected transports . . .) (*Tartuffe* I. vi); and on the other, we have the triumphant deceptions of Tartuffe himself, most triumphant over those he deludes when he is really being most truthful about himself:

> Oui, mon frère, je suis un méchant, un coupable,
> Un malheureux pécheur, tout plein d'iniquité,
> Le plus grand scélérat qui jamais ait été.

(Yes, brother, I am a wicked, guilty, wretched sinner, full of iniquity, the greatest villain that ever breathed) (III. vi).[1]

Chaucer's manner is often seemingly, but only seemingly, more naïve than this. He will simply state the fact – the action or appearance (the prioress's concern with the things of the world or the friar's preference for the rich as his penitents), or he may add a reported reason or comment as in this latter case:

> To have with sike lazars aqueyntaunce:
> It is nat honest, it may nat avaunce.
> (*Canterbury Tales*, Prologue, 245–6)

Occasionally, he will underline a remark, the monk's rejection, for instance, of the life of the cloister, with his own ironical pretence of agreement:

> And I seyde his opinion was good.
> (Ibid., 183)

Gentle irony is Chaucer's most characteristic manner. There is another line in the portrait of the monk:

[1] The translations come from the Baker and Miller version, 1739 (Everyman Series, Dent).

> A manly man, to been an abbot able.
>
> '(Ibid., 167)

which reverberates with ironic suggestion. In what sense could a man 'that loved venerye' be suitable to lead a monastic household? But before we can answer that question we are confronted with the thought, supported by what the portrait of the prioress has already suggested about the state of the ecclesiastical orders, that, as things went then, he probably was a likely candidate for the position. That word 'manly' is also suspicious; 'manly' – not 'godly', nor 'good' and 'holy' as the poor parson is later described.

But very little disturbed the balance of Chaucer's temper. He is almost always generous. By contrast we have the sardonic criticism of Clough in 'The Latest Decalogue' in which he turned with cool savagery on the Victorian age and showed how its respectable lip-service to the commandments was observance of the letter at the expense of the spirit, and, it is implied, at a cost in human suffering:

> Thou shalt not kill; but need'st not strive
> Officiously to keep alive.
> Do not adultery commit;
> Advantage rarely comes of it.
> Thou shalt not steal; an empty feat
> When it's so lucrative to cheat ...
>
> The sum of all is, thou shalt love,
> If anybody, God above:
> At any rate shall never labour
> *More* than thyself to love thy neighbour.
>
> (10–15, 21–4)

As a last example there is Milton's bitter denunciation, plain invective, against

> such as for their bellies' sake
> Creep and intrude, and climb into the fold! ...
> Blind mouths! that scarce themselves know how to hold
> A sheep-hook ...   (*Lycidas*, 114–15, 119–20)

The satirist can usually leave his victims to writhe beneath the lash of his words. The passion that produces invective is rarely content to stop at this, and so Milton, as he contemplates 'the hungry sheep [who] look up and are not fed', with ferocious glee announces that

> that two-handed engine at the door,
> Stands ready to smite once, and smite no more.

> (Ibid., 130–1)

Here we have crossed the frontiers of satire.

With religion, sex is a subject so serious that we need to seek relief in humour about it. Pre-eminent among humorous considerations of sex is Rabelais's great third book of *Gargantua and Pantagruel*. Panurge wonders whether to marry. He asks Pantagruel for advice and then he seeks a decision by random consultation of Virgil and Homer, by dice, dreams and the sibyl of Panzoult and by the advice of friends and acquaintances. The whole affair is indecisively drawn out with Rabelais maintaining a fine balance between superficial triviality and underlying seriousness. Panurge finally consults a theologian, a physician, a lawyer and a philosopher. Rabelais takes this opportunity to satirize the characteristic attitudes of members of these professions, but he is never distracted by particular or specialized satiric opportunities. He keeps his eye on universal human attitudes. The interview with the doctor Rondibilis concludes with his mock-unwillingness to accept payment. Nevertheless, he takes the money with a compliment:

> – De meschantes gens jamais je ne prens rien; rien jamais des gens de bien je ne refuse. Je suys tousjours à vostre commendement.
> (I take nothing from evil folk; I refuse nothing from good folk. I am always at your service.)

But Rabelais adds:

> – En poyant, dist Panurge.
> – Cela s'entend, respondit Rondibilis.

('Provided I pay?' said Panurge.

'That goes without saying,' Rondibilis answered.)

(*Gargantua and Pantagruel* III. 34)

Rabelais has to take everything to what he sees as the inescapable
human conclusion. Like Rabelais's, Chaucer's doctor 'lovede gold
in special'. For both writers doctors may have been avaricious, but
we have to note the truth in that final 'That goes without saying'
of Rabelais's. It is all part of the universal human condition, but it
needs descent into the absurd to convince men of it. So when
Rabelais's doctor advises on the several ways to keep down sexual
desire, he prescribes drink, drugs, work, study – and sex! (III. 31).
Cuckoldry is seen as a 'natural appendage' of wedlock (III. 32) and
'women usually hanker after forbidden things' (III. 34).

Woman's sensuality ('this beast or organ of theirs' – III. 32) is
a perennial topic of satire. It is often linked with a mock-modesty
and a concern for her reputation. Thus Chaucer's Wife of Bath
boasts both of her sexual prowess and of her skill in handling her
various husbands. The wiles of women are summed up in aban-
doned self-revelation:

> I swoor that al my walkinge out by nyghte
> Was for t'espye wenches that he dighte;
> Under that colour hadde I many a myrthe.
> For al swich wit is yeven us in our byrthe;
> Deceite, wepyng, spynnying God hath give
> To wommen kyndely, whil that they may lyve.
> And thus of o thyng I avaunte me.
> Atte ende I hadde the bettre in ech degree,
> By sleighte, or force, or by som maner thyng,
> As by continueel murmur or grucchyng.
> Namely abedde hadden they meschaunce:
> Ther wolde I chide, and do hem no plesaunce.
> (*Canterbury Tales*, The Wife of Bath's Prologue, 397–408)

The dramatic situation here is paralleled in that of Dunbar's *Tretis
of the Tua Mariit Wemen and the Wedo*, but, by contrast with the

Wife of Bath's good-humoured account, Dunbar's women are vicious and primitive in their lust. These passages are dramatic in that we are to obtain a satirical view from the speeches of characters rather than directly from the author. The theatre, especially that of the Restoration, gives us satirical comedy of situation much more complex than this. Take, for example, Wycherley's *The Country Wife*, where the libertine Horner exposes licentious women, one husband too jealous and another too lax. Not only does Horner show up these women's lust but also their concern for respectability. His pose as an eunuch enables them at once to indulge their pleasure and yet maintain their reputation. In the famous 'china' scene (IV. iii) we see also their jealousy of each other as Mrs Squeamish comes upon Lady Fidget emerging with Horner from his room after 'toiling and moiling for the prettiest piece of china, my dear'. The innuendo and *double entendre* is maintained for several lines, to be rounded off by Horner's superbly multiple-ironic reference to Mrs Squeamish: 'Alas, she has an innocent, literal understanding.' With wit more deft and delicate than Wycherley's, Congreve has Millamant prescribe the conditions by which she 'may by degrees dwindle into a wife'. The whole passage is a comprehensive statement of female humours done in a dialogue with Mirabell about what she will insist on doing and what her husband-to-be will require her not to do. The power lies in the wit, whose sharpness and surprise would not be seen again until the advent of Oscar Wilde: 'Let us be very strange and well-bred: let us be as strange as if we had been married a great while; and as well bred as if we were not married at all' (Congreve, *The Way of the World*, IV. i).

This is polished and civilized by comparison with what one finds in some of Shakespeare's remarks on women. His satire is occasional but often intense. *As You Like It* has its light-hearted mockery of the love-lorn. It also has the feigned misanthropy of Jaques. Shakespearean satire, however, finds its more characteristic note when that feigning is put aside in the all too real misanthropy of such outcasts as Lear and Timon or in the debasement of love and heroism to a world that Thersites by no means inaccurately describes as 'all wars and lechery'. Likewise, against the ideal of 'What a piece of work is a man! How noble in reason! how infinite in faculties! . . .' (*Hamlet*, II. 2), a Hamlet can see how far short of this ideal men fall – and women:

> Frailty, thy name is woman! –
> A little month. . . .
> O God! a beast that wants discourse of reason
> Would have mourn'd longer.

> (I. ii. 146–7, 150–1)

But Shakespeare does not write satirical plays and the dramatic relevance of his speeches is so direct and concentrated that the satiric importance is often subsidiary, as it is here. In some ways, the less the importance of a character, the more evident the satire. In the case of a Hamlet the anti-feminism is just part of a much broader and richer characterization, whereas with a Thersites 'all wars and lechery' is all.

The satirists do not confine themselves to the sexual behaviour of woman; others of her foibles attract their attention. Pope, for instance, in *Epistles to Several Persons* II – 'Of the Characters of Women', discourses of her unpredictability and variety. Mackail called Juvenal's sixth satire his 'Legend of Bad Women'; it is a title to suit Pope's poem as well. He considers women ruled by 'The Love of Pleasure, and the Love of Sway' (l. 210):

> Men, some to Bus'ness, some to Pleasure take;
> But ev'ry Woman is at heart a Rake;
> Men, some to Quiet, some to public Strife;
> But ev'ry Lady would be Queen for life.

> (215–18)

No wonder he accepts that '"Most Women have no Characters at all"' (2). Even as he addresses the lady to whom the poem is dedicated in the final lines he says: 'Woman's at best a Contradiction still' (270). This, however, is as nothing beside Swift's horrified misogyny. In his case, however, it was linked with a horror of the flesh as both his fascinated references to the repulsiveness of the Brobdingnagian women and the poem 'On A Beautiful Young Nymph Going to Bed' make only too apparent. The whole poem is a refutation of the normal meaning of the word 'beautiful' in the title and an insistent emphasis on the narrow connotation of 'nymph'. One function of satire is to confront us with a thing and to say 'It is not what it seems. Look!' No one has done this so thoroughly as Swift, so thoroughly indeed that the realism almost makes us forget the satire. His concentration upon the physically horrible is all but unbearable.

Swift could be complimentary and indulge a playful wit:

> STELLA this Day is Thirty-four,
> (We shan't dispute a Year or more):
> However *Stella*, be not troubled,
> Although thy Size and Years are doubled,
> Since first I saw thee at Sixteen,
> The brightest Virgin on the Green,
> So little is thy Form declin'd;
> Made up so largely in thy Mind.
> Oh! would it please the Gods to *split*
> Thy Beauty, Size, and Years, and Wit;
> No Age could furnish out a Pair
> Of Nymphs so graceful, wise, and fair:
> With half the Lustre of your Eyes,
> With half your Wit, your Years, and Size.
>
> ('Stella's Birthday', 1718, 1–14)

This is the satirist at play, reminding us in the concessive role of the fourth line that a compliment may be turned all the more neatly by glancing at a shortcoming – and reminding us also that even in such moments Swift could not escape his obsession with the physically less than beautiful.

The playfulness of the satirist is best exemplified in Pope's *The Rape of the Lock*, that apotheosis of the trivial. The quarrel that arose from the young Lord Petre's snipping off a lock of Arabella Fermor's hair had estranged the two families. The whole affair had been distorted, so Pope employed a little gentle ridicule to bring it back into proportion. His method might be described as homoeopathic. The families had exaggerated the matter, so he exaggerated it still more. He pretends that the superficialities of aristocratic society are of surpassing importance:

> Hither the Heroes and the Nymphs resort,
> To taste awhile the Pleasures of a Court;
> In various Talk th' instructive hours they past,
> Who gave the *Ball*, or paid the *Visit* last.
>
> (Canto III, 9–12)

There is a weight of irony in that word 'instructive'. Pope gently ridicules the flippant, but there is much more than this in the poem. The point can be most economically made by a look at his use of zeugma. The heroine Belinda's protecting sylph is worried about the threat to her from

> Some dire Disaster, or by Force, or Slight,
> But what, or where, the Fates have wrapt in Night.
> Whether the Nymph shall break *Diana*'s Law,
> Or some frail *China* Jar receive a flaw;
> Or stain her Honour, or her new Brocade;
> Forget her Pray'rs or miss a Masquerade.
>
> (Canto II, 103–8)

Without distinction of importance the loss of chastity is placed beside the cracking of an ornament and the staining of a dress. In one line a whole society's distorted values are exposed. The word 'rape' in the title stresses the ridiculous exaggeration of the incident; it reminds us also of matters far more important but about which there is no outcry. *The Rape of the Lock* is only apparently flippant; it is fundamentally a serious poem about right values and, in particular, about chastity.

In this section I have tried to show the satirist's function in dealing with certain topics which are central in human experience. I would end, however, by reiterating Juvenal – 'quidquid agunt homines'; anything is potential grist to the satirist's mill. He is primarily concerned not with something in itself, but with man's attitude to that thing. When man gets it out of proportion, the satirist must correct him. He restores us to sanity by making us laugh, sometimes generously, sometimes grimly. We should be able to enjoy even his anger. His correction may involve a compensating disproportion, but, provided that this is not extreme, we see its purpose and appreciate its effect.

3
Modes and Means

When we turn to the modes of satire we find that these are as various as its subjects. Few indeed are the literary forms that cannot accommodate at least a touch of satire, for satire is not only a chameleon adapting itself to its environment, it is capable of apparent metamorphosis, masquerading by parody in the very form it is criticizing. We can, in fact, turn Dryden's own satiric remarks about Flecknoe in such a way as to give them a serious meaning he did not intend and claim that satire

> In prose and verse is owned without dispute
> Through all the realms of Nonsense absolute,

for where it appears, its presence easily dominates, it is hard to eradicate and it turns whatever was before into its own form of nonsense by which its meaning is made known. We have already seen a number of its occurrences in verse, but in prose also it is found in the drama of Jonson and Congreve, Shaw and Wilde, in the works of our greatest novelists – Fielding, Jane Austen, Dickens, Thackeray, Meredith and, among lesser writers, Peacock and Evelyn Waugh, Huxley and Orwell, to mention but a few. It even occurs in historical writing, as any reader of Gibbon will know.

But this list will immediately remind us that in itself it does not take us very far. We need to make a number of distinctions to suggest the varying qualities and satiric character of these writers. This requires us to consider such matters as overall form, detailed modes of disposition and conduct of the work, and the handling of verbal, syntactical and, in the case of verse, metrical devices.

SATIRIC AND IRONIC PROCEDURES IN THE NOVEL

Some works may resemble others so extensively and persistently as to be classifiable as travesty, parody or burlesque. In others the satire may be less pervading, more partial, and perhaps more concentrated. One could here make a distinction, say, between Jane Austen's *Northanger Abbey* with its constant ridiculous recollections of the Gothic novels she is parodying and the much more incidental satire of a Dickens novel, or, perhaps better still, between the earlier parts of *Joseph Andrews* parodying Richardson's *Pamela* and the later where Fielding outgrows this limited intention and develops a broader satire and a novel that contains essentially non-satiric elements. There are well-defined satiric forms, some of which are listed in the first sentence of this paragraph. The novel, however, is so amorphous that few, if any, of its examples will fit a classification very comfortably. *Northanger Abbey* does after a fashion, so does the sustained burlesque of Evelyn Waugh's *The Loved One* with its satire on the funerary paraphernalia of affluent American society. More generally, however, we detect in the novel not the search after effect through form so much as through tone. The author so conceives his subject (and the same is true of the drama) that he then arranges his characters and incidents in relation one to another with the object of obtaining the maximum satirical effect. If he is Peacock, he will rely on speech and dialogue almost entirely. The dramatic framework is often little more than a dinner-party to bring the characters together. If he is Jonson or Congreve or any Restoration dramatist, he will wind his plot up to such a degree of complication that almost every appearance will involve the characters in a subterfuge, a contradiction between appearance and what the audience knows to be the reality, and in this way the satiric effect will be obtained. This is the mode of the drama which cannot afford to waste any opportunity in either words or action.

The novelist can be more leisurely, but even he in his role as satirist must be careful here. He must work hard. Satire ever demands the point concisely or the power intensely. This is where overall form and overall tone can help. The low intensity of an incident or isolated passage can be carried by the reader's feeling as it has been conditioned by these overall factors. Nevertheless, the occasion must be improved wherever it offers. The values of a whole society can be castigated in a well-placed parenthesis, as Fielding showed when describing a coach coming upon Joseph Andrews robbed and stripped naked. None of the comfortable occupants would help and Joseph 'must have perished, unless the postillion (a lad who hath been since transported for robbing a hen-roost) had voluntarily stripped off a greatcoat, his only garment' (*Joseph Andrews*, Bk. I, Ch. 12).

Allowing that drama (and here I include the novel) is, in Aristotelian terms, character in action, we have at least four ways by which the satiric meaning may emerge, namely, by what a man does (or fails to do), by what others do to and say of him, by what he says of himself, and, in the novel, by what the author says of him. The occupants of Fielding's coach are condemned by what they fail to do. In the same novel Parson Trulliber is condemned by what he does, by his unchristian reception of his fellow cleric, Parson Adams, in his need; but if that were all, the incident would be more moral than satiric. The criticism in this instance emerges from an episode which forms a whole comedy of errors. Fielding gives us some initial guidance by telling us that Trulliber was more pig-farmer than parson and that physically he was a grotesquely coarse caricature of a man:

> He was indeed one of the largest men you should see ... The rotundity of his belly was considerably increased by the shortness of his stature ... His voice was loud and hoarse, and his accents extremely broad. To complete the whole, he had a stateliness in his gait when he walked, not unlike that of a goose, only he stalked slower.
> (Ibid., Bk II, Ch. 14)

Here is what the author says of his character. Such is the man that the naïve and unworldly Adams is to meet, but Fielding immediately increases the possibilities of the meeting by introducing a misunderstanding. Trulliber thinks that Adams is a pig-dealer and pushes him into the pen, where 'laying hold on one of their tails, the unruly beast gave such a sudden spring, that he threw poor Adams all along in the mire. Trulliber instead of assisting him to get up, burst into a laughter.' Why do *we* laugh? Surely Adams does not deserve this. This is true, but what is happening here is happening because Fielding has a greater and a lesser satiric object. Here is what others do to and say of a character, but it is, in fact, going on in both directions. The novelist is displaying Trulliber's coarseness in action and Adams's naïveté in suffering.

The misunderstanding is resolved and the two resort to breakfast, at which, after more ill-mannered behaviour from Trulliber, Adams eventually makes his request for a loan, the real object of his visit. In a superb succession of examples of the unlikely, examples incidentally which Fielding uses to satirize contemporary society, he seeks to parallel Trulliber's astonishment:

> At last he burst forth in the following accents: 'Sir, I believe I know where to lay up my little treasure as well as another. I thank G—, if I am not so warm as some, I am content; that is a blessing greater than riches; and he to whom that is given need ask no more. To be content with a little is greater than to possess the world; which a man may possess without being so. Lay up my treasure! what matters where a man's treasure is whose heart is in the Scriptures? there is the treasure of a Christian.'

Here is what the character says of himself. We, of course, take these pulpit platitudes for what they are worth, but the real parson, as we would expect, again misunderstands. With the resolution of this misunderstanding Parson Adams brings out Trulliber's hypocrisy explicitly for what it is.

What Fielding does here with an episode he develops with all the richness and complexity of a symphony in his novels as a whole, and especially in *Tom Jones*. Characters are conceived and developed in various degrees of intimacy, depth and seriousness and exploited in comparable degrees of participation. A satiric author can be critical, yet generously critical. Fielding is so with Adams and with Tom Jones himself. Within these terms he can provide a full-length portrait or a single-angle view. The generous caricature is a rarity, and for the best of these we must go to Dickens, to such creations as Micawber with his ill-founded but irrepressible optimism that something will turn up, or in the same book, *David Copperfield*, to Mr Dick. Fielding is more severe. With him (and I exclude Parson Adams, for he is more than a caricature) the more characteristic creation is a Trulliber or a Thwackum or Square. These latter characters are respectively personifications of an extreme Evangelical and a Deistic point of view. They are rather too theoretically and narrowly conceived (see *Tom Jones*, Book III, Ch. 3), but in their actions they do nevertheless work out satisfactorily Fielding's thesis that 'Thwackum too much neglected virtue, and Square, religion, in the composition of their several systems, and . . . both utterly discarded all natural goodness of heart' (ibid., Ch. 4). They illustrate the danger of making an imaginative creation subservient to an intellectual or moral purpose. This is always a danger for the satirist. He is constantly required to maintain a fine balance between literature and life. When he fails, he can so easily decline into the mere preacher or moralist.

Nevertheless, Thwackum and Square do illustrate one aspect of the richness of *Tom Jones* and they do directly relate to the great positive value that the novel propounds, 'natural goodness of heart'. The work as a whole provides a spectrum of response to this value, ranging from the virtue of Allworthy across to the total hypocrisy of Blifil, from the good through the erring to the evil. Many of the positions within the spectrum are also reinforced by repetition. A different set of circumstances will throw up a different set of characters, but relationships and parallels are traceable, and after the manner of the picaresque novel there is the constant presence of the hero himself, erring but good-hearted Tom, responding to the subtly varied situations in which he finds himself. A novel of similar richness, but through its heroine's, if we may so describe her, pursuing a different course, is Thackeray's *Vanity Fair*. Perhaps it is better to call Becky Sharp an anti-heroine in the same way that Jonson's Volpone is an anti-hero. Both are rogues among fools, but in each case the fools are rogues until they meet in Becky and Volpone a rogue greater than themselves. In these two characters there is a certain magnificence of roguery. The history of each, however, is different. Both go from success to success, Volpone with a dazzling daring as each new piece of ingenuity outdoes its predecessor. He is an artist in crime, whose fall comes only when rogues disagree and his servant Mosca seeks to outdo his master. Volpone's empire collapses like a pack of cards, as we for long have feared it would but with each new success have wondered more and more about the likelihood of such a disaster. Becky Sharp's world, appropriately in a novel, is more prosaic. As she moves from one area of Regency society to another, Thackeray shows that Vanity Fair is everywhere. Everybody is seeking his own end and it is usually not a very noble end that each has in mind. Money is a dominating consideration, and, for enough of the men, so is sex. Even the more sympathetic characters like Dobbin are victims of their illusions about what is good, admirable and worthwhile. Jonson works by intensity of effect, Thackeray by accumulation. The first part of the novel scintillates with the ingenuity and success of Becky, but her gulls are dull rogues, and when in the later stages Becky's own appeal wanes, one realizes that the novel is monotonous, producing an evenness of effect rather than a variety. This is emphasized by the increasing unpleasantness of Becky. Whereas *Volpone* constantly

Description often implies criticism. Cf. Tolstoy's 'descriptions'!

exhilarates, *Vanity Fair* goes sour. This is a description, not a criticism. Like *Tom Jones*, it is a picaresque novel deriving its unity from the adventures of the heroine in her different circumstances, but it is a darker satire than Fielding's work. Goodness cannot find a place. *Vanity Fair* is a disillusioning book, amply confirming by its accumulation of effect the author's text with which he ends the novel:

> Ah! *Vanitas Vanitatum!* which of us is happy in this world? Which of us has his desire? or having it, is satisfied?

SATIRIC ALLEGORIES (CRIMINAL BIOGRAPHY, BEAST-FABLE, UTOPIA, JOURNEYS, BIBLICAL PARALLEL)

In *Tom Jones* and *Vanity Fair* the satire is pervasive. They are satiric novels. There are other novels in which the satire is established through the form that the novel takes, or more likely, imitates. I have mentioned the element of parody in *Northanger Abbey*, but that is a novel imitating another sort of novel. There are also works, not necessarily novels and not necessarily in prose, though many are, that are better defined as satiric allegories. Amongst these we can number criminal biography, beast-fables, utopian fantasies, imaginary journeys and biblical parallels. All these contain, in greater or lesser degree, an element of parody, but the effect that is sought is not simply that of imitation with exaggeration to emphasize the weaknesses or incongruities of the original. This original is used for other purposes, often as a norm. Parody criticizes its original; these allegories employ their originals to emphasize their own real satiric object.

They may do the first as well as the second. One book that does is Fielding's *Jonathan Wild* or, to give it its full title, *The History of the Life of the Late Mr Jonathan Wild the Great*. Every age seems to have taken a certain vicarious satisfaction from hearing about the lives and works of notable criminals. A century after

Fielding there was the 'Newgate novel' of Ainsworth and Lytton
(and even *Oliver Twist* has something of this character), which
Thackeray satirized in *Barry Lyndon*. Such a taste persists today in
the cinema. The criminal activities of Jonathan Wild, a great
organizer rather than a working thief, having things stolen and
then restoring them to their owners for a price, made a similar
appeal when Wild was tried and executed in 1725. There was a
spate of 'pot-boiling' publications, including one from Defoe.
Jonathan Wild is then, in the first place, a reflection on such
literature and its readers. It is a comment on their sense of values
in choosing to bestow a quite spurious glorification on such an
utter rogue. Its mode of proceeding is ironic. It pretends to glorify
Wild as a hero, an example of true greatness. After the manner of
irony, however, by its insistence and exaggeration it goes too far.
When Wild has a pang of conscience about the imminent execution
of Heartfree, convicted falsely by his scheming,

> He then paused a moment; but greatness, instantly returning to his
> assistance, checked the base thought, as it first offered itself to his
> mind. He then reasoned thus coolly with himself: '... Shall I, to redeem
> the worthless life of this silly fellow, suffer my reputation to contract a
> stain which the blood of millions cannot wipe away? ... What is the
> life of a single man? Have not whole armies and nations been sacrificed
> to the honour of ONE GREAT MAN? Nay, to omit that first class of
> greatness, the conquerors of mankind, how often have numbers fallen
> by a fictitious plot only to satisfy the spleen, or perhaps exercise the
> ingenuity, of a member of that second order of greatness the minis-
> terial! What have I done then? Why, I have ruined a family, and
> brought an innocent man to the gallows. I ought rather to weep with
> Alexander that I have ruined no more, than to regret the little I have
> done.'

> (Book IV, Ch. 4)

Fielding then 'apologizes' for Wild:

> [Nature] seldom creates any man so completely great, or completely
> low, but that some sparks of humanity will glimmer in the former,

and some sparks of what the vulgar call evil will dart forth in the latter.

The topsy-turvydom of values is evident enough in this comment. Wild's speech, however, takes us further – to an awareness of the number of levels at which the satire is operating. It is not only an ironic eulogy of a criminal, by which the destructive evil of his ways may be made clear. That criminal is himself a representative of what is dignified by names of honour and marks of respect elsewhere in society. Like Gay's *The Beggar's Opera*, another mock-eulogy of the criminal classes, *Jonathan Wild* was a satire on Walpole, whose conduct of affairs was notorious for its venality. He belongs to 'that second order of greatness the ministerial', and how neatly Fielding there adds a further shaft of satire, merely 'that second order'. But Fielding is also making the point that there is something worse than this, the careless disregard for men's lives that conquerors have shown in all ages. His example here is Alexander; seventy years later Byron would choose in indignant disgust 'the crowning carnage, Waterloo' (*The Vision of Judgment*, 37), and, nearer our own day, Siegfried Sassoon would sardonically reflect on the good will of the soldiers towards the general by whose inept strategy they were soon to die:

> 'Good morning; good morning!' the General said
> When we met him last week on our way to the line.
> Now the soldiers he smiled at are most of 'em dead,
> And we're cursing his staff for incompetent swine.
> 'He's a cheery old card,' grunted Harry to Jack
> As they slogged up to Arras with rifle and pack.
>
> . . . . . .
> But he did for them both by his plan of attack.
>
> ('The General')

Sassoon has added a layer; here greatness is incompetent.

The second of the forms mentioned above, the beast-fable, has a history going back satirically to Aristophanes' *Birds* and *Frogs*.

Amongst the best examples in English are Chaucer's *The Nun's Priest's Tale*, Dryden's *The Hind and the Panther* and Orwell's *Animal Farm*. In Chaucer the priest aptly tells a moral tale; his beast-fable acts as a sermon. But the form he has taken ensures that his method is not that of direct preaching or moralizing. It is by the indirect, the ironic, and the satiric that effect is achieved. Chantecleer is a strutting, sensual cock who nearly meets his doom, and though the priest disclaims high theology:

> I wol not han to do of swich matere;
> My tale is of a cok, as ye may heere,
>
> (431–2)

he nevertheless ends:

> But ye that holden this tale a folye,
> As of a fox, or of a cok and hen,
> Taketh the moralite, goode men.   (617–19)

Pride and sensuality in the cock is ridiculous. The satire is in the parallel; man is no better.

Dryden's use of the beast-fable convention is not so rich. He employs it for controversial purposes; his milk-white hind is the pure Roman Catholic Church, his spotted panther the Church of England, and the whole poem a debate on the positions of the two churches, with some additional allegorical beasts to represent various types of dissent. These figures are in one respect mere mouthpieces, in another convenient satiric characterization. Their brutal features and behaviour are applied to the sects they signify. Thus for the Presbyterians,

> More haughty than the rest, the wolfish race
> Appear with belly gaunt, and famished face:
> Never was so deformed a beast of grace.
> His ragged tail betwixt his legs he wears,
> Close clipped for shame; but his rough crest he rears,
> And pricks up his predestinating ears.
>
> (I. 160–5)

Dryden's equivalences, however, are sparse and arbitrary beside the brilliant appropriateness of Swift's application to differing religious views of the clothes parallel in *A Tale of a Tub* – first Peter (the Roman Church) adding ornament to his father's coat which he had inherited, and then Martin [Luther] (the Church of England) discarding prudently, and Jack [Calvin] (the Dissenters) tearing carelessly and damaging both decoration and clothing indiscriminately. But Swift also goes beyond this single parallel, as, for instance, in the following:

> 'Bread,' says [Peter], 'dear brothers, is the staff of life; in which bread is contained, inclusive, the quintessence of beef, mutton, veal [&c.]. Upon the strength of these conclusions, next day at dinner was the brown loaf served up in all the formality of a city feast. 'Come, brothers,' said Peter, 'fall to, and spare not; here is excellent good mutton.'
>
> (Section IV)

Thus Swift represents transubstantiation. It is not merely, however, in the dexterity of application that the difference between Swift and Dryden consists; it is also in the informing tone of the whole. Swift is more witty and less ponderous, more daring and less conventional than Dryden.

Orwell more closely resembles Swift in his sustained closeness of application of comparison to subject, vehicle to tenor, in *Animal Farm*, proceeding as he does from the revolution of the farm animals against their human master through an idealistic phase of egalitarianism to the usurpation of power by the pigs and the ultimate dictatorship of one of them, Napoleon. Stage by stage there are parallels with the history of Soviet Russia, but, like Fielding in *Jonathan Wild*, Orwell makes this, more than an incidental satire, into a blast against political tyranny based on the subversion of idealism anywhere at any time. Its contemporary application, however, makes it an excellent example to bear out I. A. Richards's view that 'vehicle and tenor in co-operation give a

meaning of more varied powers than can be ascribed to either'
(*The Philosophy of Rhetoric*, London, 1936, p. 100); each enriches
the other by cumulative interpenetration. One can see this, for
instance, in the successive impositions of double-talk on the
original simple seven commandments. As the pigs progressively
imitate men, so each commandment is modified. When they take
to occupying the beds in the farm-house, 'No animal shall sleep in
a bed' becomes 'No animal shall sleep in a bed *with sheets*'. The final
betrayal comes with the modification of the last and greatest commandment 'All animals are equal' to read 'All animals are equal but
some animals are more equal than others.' The different animals
are so many different versions of the human condition, but each is
affected as an individual, and thus we gain the impression not of
'a fairy story', as the novel is sub-titled, but of a vast and realistic
social catastrophe which gives to this sub-title the savage irony
that Orwell surely intended.

Eugene Ionesco also uses the beast-fable device for a political
satiric allegory. His *Rhinoceros* (1960) shows the whole population
of a town changed into rhinoceroses. This is the author's equi-
valent of the various forms of collective hysteria that have resulted
from totalitarian indoctrination in this century. Like Orwell's *1984*
the play uses one character, Berenger, to resist and to criticize. At
the end he pathetically confesses:

> Trop tard maintenant! Hélas, je suis un monstre, je suis un monstre.
> Hélas, jamais je ne deviendrai rhinocéros, jamais, jamais!
>
> (Now it's too late! Now I'm a monster, just a monster. Now I'll never
> become a rhinoceros, never, never.)

but he recovers in the last sentence

> Je suis le dernier homme, je le resterai jusqu'au bout! Je ne capitule
> pas!
>
> (I'm the last man left, and I'm staying that way until the end. I'm not
> capitulating.)[1]

[1] These translations are taken from the Penguin version of the play.

Animal Farm and *Rhinoceros* are closed worlds. So are the Utopias which various writers have constructed – More's *Utopia*, Butler's *Erewhon*, Morris's *News from Nowhere*, Huxley's *Brave New World*, Orwell's *1984*, to name but a few. The utopian idea goes back to Plato's dream of an ideal state in his *Republic*. The utopian fantasy, however, does not look necessarily to an ideal condition. The vision may be one which the author thinks will constitute a community of happiness, but it may, as with Huxley, be not real but synthetic happiness. It may even, as with *1984*, be some people's idea of Utopia in which individuals are, in fact, made to suffer. In this respect the two last works on my list provide interesting and significant variations on the other three. Each of these latter grew out of an idealism which was at odds with the shortcomings of the author's own society. When More extols communism and forbids private property, he has in mind the 'conspiracy of the rich against the poor', which in his time was manifested in land enclosure, rural depopulation and widespread unemployment and starvation, but his criticism and remedy go beyond this, embracing a condemnation of war, religious persecution, harsh legal penalties and even bad housing. For Butler everything is wrong way round. Erewhon itself is a reversed anagram of Nowhere. It is a place where crime is treated as illness and illness as crime, where the Church is a Bank for laying up treasure in heaven by good pretension, where women worship the godless Ydgrun (Mrs Grundy). Butler is more light-hearted than More, perhaps less serious, but each – Butler by inversion and More by substitution and contrast – provides a telling satire on his contemporary society.

These are hopeful satirists; they could propound a remedy. Huxley and Orwell in our own century are much less sanguine. Theirs are negative Utopias in which the cure is worse than the disease. Huxley gives us in *Brave New World*, an early example of science fiction, a society in which human relationships have been superseded by scientific disposition. The satirist has often laughed at the scientist. The first Samuel Butler's *The Elephant in the Moon* turns astronomers' excitement into uproarious farce. The early years of the Royal Society also provided matter for Pope (e.g. the contest of the carnation-cultivator and the butterfly-collector in *The Dunciad*, Book IV) and Swift who in his description of the Academy of Lagado attacked sterile, useless experiments of the kind which sought to extract sunbeams from cucumbers and to build houses from the roof downwards (*Gulliver's Travels*, Part III, Ch. 5). Swift's reactions provide a most sensitive barometer to the danger he sees in what he satirizes. The academic projectors are the butts of only comparatively light ridicule. Swift saw no real danger in science; only that a lot of it was rather silly. Huxley cannot be so genial about it. For him our mechanical, technological civilization is full of dangers. He sees in scientific breeding and the deity of the Almighty Ford, to mention but two of his horrid fantasies, the dehumanization of man. The burden of Orwell's fear, by contrast, is the depersonalization of the individual. *1984* is a pessimistic extension of *Animal Farm* in which every individual is all the time aware that 'Big Brother' is watching him, in which all are subjected to the intrusive tyranny of the two-way television set and in which each person has an inescapable role and function in society, against which there can be no effectual revolt. The book is a sustained and terrifying portrayal of the ultimate horror for the individual in a politically authoritarian and technologically dominated society.

There are those who have identified Swift's Utopia with his description of the Houyhnhnms in the fourth book of *Gulliver's Travels*. The controversy as to whether this is so or not is too complicated to be entered upon here. (The interested reader is directed to R. Quintana's *The Mind and Art of Jonathan Swift*, revd. London, 1953, F. R. Leavis's essay in *The Common Pursuit*, London, 1952, I. Ehrenpreis's *The Personality of Jonathan Swift*,

London, 1958, and the criticism of the last-named's view in R. S. Crane's contribution to J. A. Mazzeo's *Reason and the Imagination*, London, 1962.) For our purposes *Gulliver's Travels* illustrates yet another form of the satiric allegory, the imaginary journey. In its first two books it also displays another satiric device, that of criticism through relative size. By means of the journey the author (or his main character – and of this something later) is able to exploit the circumstances expressed in the adage *autre pays, autres moeurs*, but he may find that it is a case also of *plus ça change, plus c'est la même chose*; he can work, that is, by either simple contrast, or apparent difference but basic similarity, or both. He can even go beyond that by positing a situation to which neither of the compared societies conforms. This Swift does in the sixth chapter of the voyage to Lilliput (Part I) where he sets out an ideal constitution of learning, laws and customs which, however, he qualifies by saying that this represents 'the original institutions, and not the most scandalous corruptions into which these people are fallen by the degenerate nature of man'. Instead, the Lilliputians re-enact some of the more despicable of human (and English) manners in, for example, the controversy about breaking eggs between the Big Endians and Little Endians, parodying the religious quarrels of Roman Catholics and Anglicans, or again in the acrobatic antics of those who seek political promotion. The minuteness of the Lilliputians adds point to the satire, whilst at the same time giving to Gulliver in his recognition of their ridiculous behaviour a representative role as a superior sensible human being. The tables are turned when in the next book Swift exploits the discrepancy of size at the expense of humanity. Nor does he simply reverse man's position. Gulliver's behaviour in Brobdingnag is, if anything, worse than that of the Lilliputians, especially when, with the size of an insect in the presence of the king, he not only describes but openly boasts about the obviously corrupt, if not outright evil, human management of war, law, government and finance. This is

Swift's deep irony at work. He rounds the scene off with a departure from the oblique, a shocking incursion into positive condemnation with the king's summary of the whole matter: 'I cannot but conclude the bulk of your natives, to be the most pernicious race of little odious vermin that nature ever suffered to crawl upon the surface of the earth' (Part II, Ch. 6). Gulliver, however, is undaunted in his arrogance and goes on to criticize Brobdingnagian institutions and practice – 'the miserable effects of a *confined education*', 'a strange effect of *narrow principles* and *short views*', etc. We have come to the point of the author (or his main character). Gulliver is now a blind hero, the vehicle for his creator's ironic criticism. But Gulliver represents mankind equally in both the first two books, in the first enabling us to appreciate the satire of apparent difference but basic similarity, in the second that of simple contrast. This is, in fact, an oversimplification, especially of Brobdingnag, for there are hints, if nothing more, of Swift's critical attitude to this giant-people, and there are certainly signs of his disgust at their physical crudity. This disgust he concentrated in the symbol of the Yahoos, the man-like apes of the fourth book, personifications of bestiality, who contrast with the intelligent and humane horses, the Houyhnhnms. In these latter we may have an instance of the satiric inadequate ideal, creatures who appear better than they are, who are certainly taken for ideal by Gulliver himself. There are signs, however, especially after he leaves them and returns to humanity, that they are not really as wonderful as he thinks them or, more accurately, that Swift shows Gulliver's judgement as distorted. Much of the difficulty and difference in the interpretation of this last book may arise from the fact that Swift's signposts are too subtly painted or, more serious still, that they are in the wrong places. There seems much to be said for the elegance of R. S. Crane's argument based as it is on a simple inversion of the roles of man and animal which Swift had found in the logic text-books of his student days.

Swift's work reminds us that it is not just the place but also the person who may reveal the author's satiric angle. Gulliver meets the King of Brobdingnag as an arrogant sophisticate confronting an ignorant primitive creature. Thereby Swift reveals the goodness and wisdom of innocence. Fielding in *Joseph Andrews* achieves the same effect through Parson Adams, descendant of Cervantes' Don Quixote. Both works in which these characters appear began with intentions other than those they eventually assume. Cervantes begins by deflating chivalric romance, Fielding by ridiculing Richardson's sentimentality and prudential view of virtue. Each, however, goes on with characters who view the world as little children. Quixote and Adams are innocents and they bear the buffets of reality for their innocence. At the end, however, the world of experience is the worse in the reader's eyes for the criticism they have brought to bear upon it. An alternative version of the innocent eye is the device of the foreign visitor. Thus Voltaire's Candide marvels at (and is horrified by) the ways of the English in the shooting of Admiral Byng:

> Mais dans ce pays-ci il est bon de tuer de temps en temps un amiral pour encourager les autres.

> (But in this country it is advisable now and then to kill an admiral, in order to encourage the others.)

> (*Candide*, Ch. 22)

Goldsmith's Chinese visitor and Montesquieu's traveller in *Les Lettres Persanes* likewise bring a fresh and even naïve but thereby critical eye on the societies in which they find themselves. Heine in *Deutschland. Ein Wintermärchen* uses both place and time – place through the viewpoint of a man re-visiting his native land, time through the tacit equation of the medieval Barbarossa with the contemporary Frederick William IV. Large parts of cantos XIV and XV seem prophetic of Prussian militarism, whilst elsewhere we read the mock-serious advice:

Behagt dir das Guillotinieren nicht,
So bleib bei den alten Mitteln:
Das Schwert für Edelleute, der Strick
Für Bürger und Bauern in Kitteln.

Nur manchmal wechsle ab, und laß
Den Adel hängen, und köpfe
Ein bißchen die Bürger und Bauern, wir sind
Ja alle Gottesgeschöpfe.

(Canto XVII)

(If you don't like guillotining, keep to the old measures: the sword for the nobility, the rope for burghers and besmocked peasants.

But make a change sometimes, and let nobles be hanged, and chop off a few burghers' and peasants' heads, we are all God's creatures.)[1]

One other form of satiric allegory remains – the biblical parallel, of which the single great example is Dryden's poem *Absalom and Achitophel*. The form was common in the seventeenth century and this particular tale was used on a number of occasions (see B. N. Schilling, *Dryden and the Conservative Myth*, New Haven, 1961). Biblical allegory offers a variety of appeal. Dryden would be able to rely on his readers' familiarity even with a fairly obscure incident, and they in their turn would appreciate the wit by which he turned both overall story and carefully selected detail so cogently to serve his own purposes. Thus in 'god-like David's' representation of Charles II Dryden was able at once to exalt the king by comparison to the lofty messianic monarch of Old Testament days and to use David's well-attested sexual appetite ingeniously to pass over Charles's similar propensity. He can even use both the minimal characters of the Old Testament who bear the name of Zimri, each to contribute something appropriate to his own Zimri, the Duke of Buckingham. The one was lover of Cozbi (Numbers xxv); of the other, son of Elah, it was asked 'Had Zimri peace who slew his master?' (2 Kings ix. 31). From the two

[1] Translation from *Heine* by Peter Branscombe, The Penguin Poets Series.

characters Dryden drew the restlessness, treasonable intent and sexual intrigue which he ascribed to Buckingham. This, however, is but one aspect of the poem, though the most obvious. It also has associations with epic and particularly with *Paradise Lost*. Thus the temptation of Absalom by Achitophel is satirically magnified by inference to that of man by Satan. Phrase and sentence-structure:

> Him staggering so when hell's dire agent found,

(373)

image:

> The joyful people thronged to see him land,
> Covering the beach, and blackening all the strand;
> But, like the prince of angels, from his height
> Comes tumbling downward with diminished light,

(271–4)

and, especially, the structure of debate and temptation give to the poem an enrichment by comparison. It is worth noting Dryden's agility in the two images of the passage above. The people who now challenge Charles are compared to the locusts who 'darkened all the land of Nile', one of Milton's images for the fallen angels (*Paradise Lost* I. 343), but, at first rather surprisingly, the next simile compares Charles to the devil himself. We have, however, to put it in the context of the whole passage. Even the preceding couplet will do. In the eyes of his people and of Achitophel, his enemy, who makes this speech, Charles *is* now the devil himself. The whole four lines show that, self-seeking conspirator as he is, Achitophel thinks well neither of the King to whom he should be faithful nor of the people whose cause he pretends to enhance.

LOW AND HIGH BURLESQUE

Satire often uses epic, though not usually in so straight a parallel as this. As the most elevated of literary forms epic offers ample scope for the distortions of satire, either by direct deflation or by oblique mock-exaltation. Both of these modes are forms of burlesque, the first, low burlesque in which, as Boileau put it, 'Dido and Aeneas are made to speak like fishwives and ruffians', the second, high burlesque or mock-epic in which, conceivably, fishwives and ruffians would speak (and act) like Dido and Aeneas. Butler's *Hudibras* is a good example of low burlesque, though of a special kind. He describes the ridiculous adventures of a Puritan knight, not in the lofty idiom suitable to knightly deeds, but in jingling verse and colloquial language. Whereas *Don Quixote* is a burlesque of chivalric romance, *Hudibras* goes a stage further and vulgarizes the mode. Thus of the hero we read:

> Chief of domestic knights and errant
> Either for chartel or for warrant;
> Great on the bench, great in the saddle,
> That could as well bind o'er as swaddle.
> Mighty he was at both of these,
> And styled of War, as well as Peace
> (So some rats of amphibious nature,
> Are either for the land or water):
> But here our authors make a doubt
> Whether he was more wise or stout:
> Some hold the one, and some the other;
> But, howsoe'er they make a pother,
> The diff'rence was so small, his brain
> Outweighed his rage but half a grain;
> Which made some take him for a tool
> That knaves do work with, called a Fool.
>
> (Part I, Canto I. 21–36)

Butler has no generosity and the mode he uses suits his temper. It is ideal for despising, and Butler is all scorn.

High burlesque, or mock-epic, can also be scornful, but it allows for other tones than this. Dryden in *MacFlecknoe* takes an epic event, a coronation, as his subject and he describes it in appropriately elevated language. The poem begins on the note of moralistic satire:

> All human things are subject to decay,
> And when fate summons, monarchs must obey.

There are lines that in isolation might come from epic itself:

> At his right hand our young Ascanius sate,
> Rome's other hope and pillar of the state.
>
> (108–9)

There is only the hint of familiarity in 'our' to disturb the suitability of this couplet as pure epic. The opening scene shows Flecknoe:

> This aged prince, now flourishing in peace,
> And blessed with issue of a large increase;
> Worn out with business, did at length debate
> To settle the succession of the state.
>
> (7–10)

Did we not know by a single (and so far unelaborated) reference that this 'aged prince' was Flecknoe, king of the dunces, this would be acceptable as an elevated statement – except perhaps for 'worn out with business'. My point is that Dryden subtly uses the tone of epic with but slight adulteration to achieve many of his effects. With this, however, he mingles elements of downright deflation. Sometimes it is the effect of a final word or phrase as when Flecknoe,

> who, like Augustus, young
> Was called to empire, and had governed long;
> In prose and verse, was owned, without dispute,
> Through all the realms of Nonsense, absolute.
>
> (3–6)

Elsewhere Dryden rams home the satire in mock-praise, especially in Flecknoe's choice of Shadwell as his successor:

> Shadwell alone my perfect image bears,
> Mature in dulness from his tender years:
> Shadwell alone, of all my sons, is he,
> Who stands confirmed in full stupidity.
>
> (15–18)

The action of the poem is slight, but it gives Dryden scope to introduce and pillory most of the bad writers of his time. Pope's *Dunciad* is more elaborate, more fully imitative of epic in its action with, for example, sacrifice to and appearance of the goddess, ceremonial games, and a visit to the underworld, all with their parallels in Virgil's *Aeneid*.

The mode of mock-heroic is not simply parody, for parody concentrates on exaggerating the style of its model and thus satirizing the model itself. Mock-heroic uses its model to satirize something else by means of the comparison, and it possesses considerable freedom in the closeness or otherwise of the comparison. It always, however, exaggerates to deflate. Pope's *The Rape of the Lock* does this with the trivialities of Belinda and her society, but, in contrast to Dryden, there is greater subtlety and delicacy. The supernatural guidance of the sylphs is at once attractive and ridiculous. Moreover, Pope is concerned not so much with the small masquerading as the great as with the criticism of misdirected qualities. This is the context of his criticism of Belinda's toilet:

> And now, unveil'd, the *Toilet* stands display'd,
> Each Silver Vase in mystic Order laid.
> First, rob'd in White, the Nymph intent adores,
> With Head uncover'd, the *Cosmetic* Pow'rs.
> A heav'nly Image in the Glass appears,
> To that she bends, to that her Eyes she rears;
> Th' inferior Priestess, at her Altar's side,
> Trembling, begins the sacred Rites of Pride.
>
> (Canto I, 121–8)

Dryden's satire is crude in tone by comparison with this, and yet this is a sustained and cumulative indictment of values so wrong that cosmetic preparations can be described in terms of religious imagery. We must be careful of being over-serious. At the same time we need to remember that many a truth is spoken in jest. The precision of Pope's tone can be measured by a comparison with Dryden on the one hand and, say, Jonson in Volpone's hymn to gold on the other, where we are horrified by the sheer blasphemy of Volpone's attitude.

We need to keep in mind Pope's versatility in *The Rape of the Lock*. The extent of satiric magnification by mock-heroic device varies from place to place. Sometimes, indeed, he appears to desert the epic connexion for more direct satire as in:

> The hungry Judges soon the Sentence sign,
> And Wretches hang that Jury-men may dine,
>
> (Canto III. 21–2)

or for simple parody, as in the speech of Sir Plume, who

> thus broke out – 'My Lord, why, what the Devil?
> Z—ds! damn the Lock! 'fore Gad, you must be civil!'
>
> (Canto IV. 127–8)

with the beautiful ironic comment:

> It grieves me much (reply'd the Peer again)
> Who speaks so well shou'd ever speak in vain.
>
> (Ibid., 131–2)

Even indeed in a parody of epic speech, indubitably an example of mock-heroism, there intrudes such a degree of moralistic comment that the ridiculous of mock-heroic takes a subsidiary place. Clarissa parodies the Sarpedon to Glaucus speech (Homer, *Iliad* XII) and, though much of the reference is on the level of the rest of the poem, the intent and conclusion are directly serious:

> Beauties in vain their pretty Eyes may roll;
> Charms strike the Sight, but Merit wins the Soul.
>
> (Canto V. 33–4)

The mock-heroic did not confine itself to poetry, as Swift's *The Battle of the Books* demonstrates. Better than in any other English imitation, Swift employs that staple event of epic, the battle, with all the vocabulary of war which is found in Homer and Virgil. In this respect his work has many of the elements of parody. There is also an element of low burlesque here, for Swift denigrates the dignity of scholarship with some of his comparisons. Thus of Bentley we read that

> His armour was patched up of a thousand incoherent pieces ... His helmet was old rusty iron ... In his right hand he grasped a flail and (that he might never be unprovided of an offensive weapon) a vessel full of ordure in his left.

We note here also the pun ('offensive') and the scatological reference. This latter is part of Swift's fascination with the repulsive, but it is not confined to him. Both Dryden and Pope (in *The Dunciad*) supply comparable examples. Wotton joins Bentley and provides the opportunity for an elaborate mock-epic simile:

> As when two mongrel curs, whom native greediness and domestic want provoke and join in partnership, though fearful, nightly to invade the folds of some rich grazier, they, with tails depressed and lolling tongues crept soft and slow.

It is not only the length and detail of the simile that reminds us of epic associations (and disparities) but also the syntactical structure of the sentence both as a whole and in detail. Swift uses the simile to contrast the two sides in the battle. Bentley and Wotton are likened to curs, but the comparison of Boyle is more appropriate to epic:

> As a young lion in the Libyan plains or Arabian desert, sent by his aged sire to hunt for prey, or health, or exercise, he scours along, wishing to meet some tiger from the mountains or a furious boar.

MacFlecknoe, The Rape of the Lock and *The Battle of the Books* should together show something of the variety of tone in high burlesque. There is the scornful and contemptuous, as I noted at the beginning, but there is also a more generous ridicule. In fact, mock-epic usually means that the author is in a fairly good temper. The very form is basically a hoax, a form of bluff. In order to succeed, the hoaxer needs to have a correct perspective. There is nothing like bad temper for producing exaggeration of the wrong kind, exaggeration that destroys perspective.

More complex than anything in the Augustan satires referred to in this section is the twentieth-century *Ulysses* of James Joyce. Its title indicates its reference back to Homer, but it is not just mock-epic. In some respects it is a story of truly epic proportions – in its range, its sensitive interpretation of human experience, its profound insight into human psychology, to name no others. Bloom is a personification of twentieth-century man, the little-man hero. In this, of course, there is an irony: Bloom now, Ulysses then. There is also plenty of incidental irony; in the Circe episode, for example, just at the critical moment Bloom recognizes reality for what it is – because his back trousers' button snaps! At times the irony reverberates, as in Bloom's fantasy-speech on social ideals in which he assumes a series of roles from working man to benevolent dictator ending with a declaration for 'free money free love and a free lay church in a free lay state' (*Ulysses*, Bodley Head edn., London, 1937, p. 466). In Bloom here there is the naïveté that believes such promises and the cynicism that knows they are just so much verbiage. Bloom is also an impostor, he pretends to be the various people he mimics; but in so doing he reduces the reality itself to a fraud. The mimicking itself is parody, an art in which Joyce was an extremely versatile performer. In the 'Oxen of the Sun' section he takes us through the history of English prose style from Old English alliterative 'Before born babe bliss had' (p. 367) through medieval Mandeville, Restoration Pepys, Augustan Addison, late eighteenth-century Burke to a mêlée of nineteenth-century styles.

For good measure much of the preceding 'Nausicaa' episode is cast in the manner of popular novelette.

'CHARACTERS' AND CHARACTERIZATION

The whole may well be more than the sum of the parts, but to appreciate the whole we need to look at the parts. We shall accordingly move now from overall form to detailed modes of disposition and conduct of satire. Satire is about people, and there must therefore be some form of characterization. The simplest form is that of description by the author. Such are the portraits of Chaucer or of Dryden. They are 'characters' in the tradition of Theophrastus (third century B.C.), who with his list of things that various people did produced a rogues' gallery. Chaucer's *Prologue* in many ways is just such another. Not all the Canterbury pilgrims are rogues but most of the memorable ones are, in greater or lesser degree. Chaucer mingles statement of fact with description of behaviour and sometimes adds to these a comment, often of ironic praise. He also leaves things unsaid or merely implied. Thus of the Friar he could write:

> A limitour, a ful solempne man,
> In alle the ordres foure is noon that can
> So muche of daliaunce and fair langage,
> He hadde maad ful many a mariage
> Of yonge wommen, at his owne cost,
> Unto his ordre he was a noble post.

> (209–14)

We notice the incongruities of 'solempne' and 'daliaunce and fair langage'. What have these latter to do with a friar? Then his arrangement of marriages – so generously 'at his owne cost'. But why? We are left to supply the shameful answer, and thus to give the succeeding comment the full weight of its ironic force.

Dryden's characters draw on a more definite literary mode,

deriving from Theophrastus, as it flourished in the seventeenth century – from the character-writing of men like Hall, Overbury and Earle. The last-named catches the mannerisms of the types he criticizes. Thus the 'pretender of learning'

> walks much alone in the posture of meditation, and has a book still before his face in the fields. His pocket is seldom without a Greek Testament or Hebrew Bible, which he opens only in the church, and that when some stander-by looks over. . . . If he read anything in the morning, it comes up all at dinner; and as long as that lasts, the discourse is his.

In *Absalom and Achitophel* Dryden exploited this mode of incisive comment within the concise epigrammatic unit of the heroic couplet. His characters, however, draw less upon action and are described more in terms of their qualities. Thus

> the false Achitophel was first;
> A name to all succeeding ages cursed:
> For close designs and crooked counsels fit;
> Sagacious, bold and turbulent of wit;
> Restless, unfixed in principles and place,
> In power unpleased, impatient of disgrace,

(150–5)

whilst Zimri was

> A man so various that he seemed to be
> Not one, but all mankind's epitome:
> Stiff in opinions, always in the wrong;
> Was everything by starts, and nothing long:
> But in the course of one revolving moon
> Was chymist, fiddler, statesman and buffoon.

(545–50)

Dryden's method is to accumulate words, to balance phrases, to suggest a complete statement within a closed couplet.

It is worth putting two other passages alongside these to illustrate another point. Of Shimei he wrote that his

> youth did early promise bring
> Of zeal to God and hatred to his king:
> Did wisely from expensive sins refrain,
> And never broke the Sabbath, but for gain,
>
> (585–8)

whilst Corah's

> long chin proved his wit; his saint-like grace
> A church-vermilion, and a Moses' face.
> His memory, miraculously great,
> Could plots, exceeding man's belief, repeat
> Which therefore cannot be accounted lies,
> For human wit could never such devise.
>
> (648–53)

It is difficult to illustrate the difference of tone by such short quotations, but I would simply point to the outright condemnation of Achitophel accompanied by the list of his capable and therefore dangerous qualities. There is a hint of fear, not least in the hissing alliteration of the second line, whereas Dryden is laughing at Zimri. In a much-quoted passage from his *Discourse Concerning Satire* he wrote of this 'character': ''Tis not bloody, but 'tis ridiculous enough.' This follows his claim: 'How easy is it to call rogue and villain, and that wittily! But how hard to make a man appear a fool, a blockhead, or a knave, without using any of these opprobrious terms.' 'The nicest and most delicate touches of satire consist in fine raillery.' That delicacy is missing in the portraits of Shimei and Corah, and in the latter there is even a coarseness that leads to caricature of the victim's physical appearance. It is alleviated somewhat by the wit that suggests that the only way to rescue Titus Oates's witness in the Popish Plot from the charge of fabrication is to assume that he is not human – and therefore perhaps devilish! There is a gradation of tone in these four passages from hate through ridicule to contempt and scorn.

There are yet other tones in Johnson's *The Vanity of Human*

Wishes. Of this poem T. S. Eliot claimed that it was '*purer* satire than anything of Dryden or Pope, nearer in spirit to the Latin. For the satirist is in theory a stern moralist castigating the vices of his time or place.' (Introduction to *Johnson's London and The Vanity of Human Wishes*, 1930). Johnson's characters are moral *exempla* of various human vanities – the pursuit of power, learning, wealth, beauty and so on. He bids us consider each of his chosen representatives:

> In full-blown dignity, see Wolsey stand,
> Law in his voice, and fortune in his hand ...
> At length his sovereign frowns ...
> At once is lost the pride of awful state,
> The golden canopy, the glittering plate ...
> Grief aids disease, remembered folly stings,
> And his last sighs reproach the faith of kings.
>
> (98–9, 109, 113–14, 119–20)

All of them serve but 'to point a moral or adorn a tale' (223). The moral is expressed simply in the fireworks image:

> They mount, they shine, evaporate and fall.   (76)

The 'character' method is a useful means for introducing a character in a novel. Thus Fielding introduces Beau Didapper:

> a young gentleman of about four foot five inches in height. He wore his own hair though the scarcity of it might have given him sufficient excuse for a periwig. His face was thin and pale; the shape of his body and legs none of the best. . . . The qualifications of his mind were well adapted to his person. . . . He was not entirely ignorant; for he could talk a little French and sing two or three Italian songs; . . . he seemed not much inclined to avarice, for he was profuse in his expenses; nor had he all the features of prodigality, for he never gave a shilling: no hater of women, for he always dangled after them; yet so little subject to lust, that he had, among those who knew him best, the character of great moderation in his pleasures . . .
>
> (*Joseph Andrews*, Book IV, Ch. 9)

Here is criticism by concessive and negative approach and by balancing one quality against another but putting both in their worst light. For a quite different method consider Dickens's portrait of Mr Bounderby:

> Mr Bounderby was as near being Mr Gradgrind's bosom friend, as a man perfectly devoid of sentiment can approach that spiritual relationship towards another man perfectly devoid of sentiment ...
>
> He was a rich man; banker, merchant, manufacturer, and what not. A big, loud man, with a stare, and a metallic laugh. A man made out of a coarse material, which seemed to have been stretched to make so much of him. A man with a great puffed head and forehead, swelled veins in his temples, and such a strained skin to his face that it seemed to hold his eyes open, and lift his eyebrows up. A man with a pervading appearance on him of being inflated like a balloon, and ready to start. A man who was always proclaiming through that brassy speaking-trumpet of a voice of his, his old ignorance and his old poverty. A man who was the Bully of humility.
>
> (*Hard Times*, Book I, Ch. 4)

This is much more strident, in keeping with the kind of character portrayed. Indeed, by this method Dickens seems to ascribe this author-summary to the voice of the character himself. We are battered by the insistent repetitions of 'A man ... A man ...' The caricature which Fielding merely hints at is here fully developed, with the added effect of the comic comparison ('like a balloon...') that comes so easily to Dickens. The fuller development of caricature and the aptly comic comparison both derive from Dickens's vivid pictorial imagination. It is this which makes Dickens, not simple, but unsubtle and direct.

Bounderby is at once an individual and a representative. He embodies some of the most callous aspects of unrestrained *laissez-faire*, but with these are united those personal qualities which pronounce him loud and overbearing. These unpleasant personal traits make the thing he represents all the more repulsive. Dickens's ability to select and apply such personal qualities gives to such characters a greater fullness and force than many other authors are able to obtain. To take an example, Peacock's Mr Toobad, the Manichaean Millenarian:

> The twelfth verse of the twelfth chapter of *Revelation* was always in his mouth: 'Woe to the inhabiters of the earth and of the sea; for the devil is come among you, having great wrath, because he knoweth that he hath but a short time.' (*Nightmare Abbey*, Ch. 1)

Peacock here picks out two aspects of doctrine – total earthly evil and apocalyptic anticipation – much stressed by some of the Evangelicals of his time, but Mr Toobad never gets beyond having these words 'always in his mouth'. He is, in fact, not a character but a satiric-comic device. Peacock relies almost exclusively on speech and dialogue, and we get better results when he can give his character rather broader terms of reference. This happens especially when he can go beyond the narrowly defined type (as in Mr Toobad) to the widely recognized individual. The well-known writer is an apt example of the latter. Thus he can satirize what he called Byron's 'atrabilarious' temperament in words that are so close to the poet's own that one hesitates to call them parody:

> We wither from our youth; we gasp with unslaked thirst for unattainable good; lured from the first to the last by phantoms – love, fame, ambition, avarice – all idle, and all ill – one meteor of many names that vanishes in the smoke of death.
>
> (Ibid., Ch. 12)

Here are Byron's words:

> We wither from our youth, we gasp away –
> Sick – sick – unfound the boon, unslaked the thirst,
> Though to the last, in verge of our decay,
> Some phantom lures such as we sought at first –
> But all too late – so are we doubly cursed.
> Love, fame, ambition, avarice – 'tis the same,
> Each idle, and all ill, and none the worst –
> For all are meteors with a different name,
> And Death the sable smoke where vanishes the flame.
>
> (*Childe Harold*, Canto IV, stanza 126)

Peacock indulges in no artificial heightening, no distortion. He simply puts verse into prose and thereby makes it look so self-conscious as to seem artificial and insincere. But Peacock does go beyond satire of words. In his criticism of Coleridge he makes that writer's satiric *alter ego*, Mr Flosky, ridicule what Peacock considered an increasing tendency to obscurantist philosophy in Coleridge. When Marionetta asks for 'a plain answer to a plain question', Flosky replies:

> It is impossible, my dear Miss O'Carroll. I never gave a plain answer to a question in my life ... [and then after a lot of verbose hair-splitting] if any person living could make report of having obtained any information on any subject from Ferdinando Flosky, my transcendental reputation would be ruined for ever.
>
> (Ibid., Ch. 8)

There is a refinement of parody when one character acts in parallel with another. Such is the function which Krook performs in *Bleak House*, where he is 'called among the neighbours the Lord Chancellor. His shop is called the Court of Chancery' (Ch. 5). He himself is 'short, cadaverous and withered', and his shop is a junk warehouse containing rubbish of every description. 'One had only to fancy ... that yonder bones in a corner, piled together and picked very clean, were the bones of clients, to make the picture complete.' (Ibid.) This is a sardonic obliqueness, a kind of symbolic satire, just as the fog and mire of London is in the first chapter:

> Never can there come fog too thick, never can there come mud and mire too deep, to assist with the groping and floundering condition which this High Court of Chancery, most pestilent of hoary sinners, holds, this day, in the sight of heaven and earth.

Fog, literal and metaphysical, actual and symbolic, surrounds the Court of Chancery. Thus by figurative parallels, or savage exten-

E

sion of parody into the realm of things, Dickens satirizes this corrupt institution.

To return to character. Sometimes we find that the character neither bears any recognizable relationship to anyone we know nor has any well-defined identity in himself. He may simply be his author's mouthpiece. This situation is found at its extreme in Wilde, where characters with the flimsiest of individual identities become the vehicles for the author's wit:

> *Jack:* I have lost both my parents.
> *Lady Bracknell:* To lose one parent, Mr Worthing, may be regarded as misfortune; to lose both looks like carelessness.
>
> (*The Importance of Being Earnest*, Act I)

Wilde is content for his wit to surprise by its epigrammatic unexpectedness. Shaw imbues much of his wit with a sharp social comment, arising from an inversion of commonplace. Thus in *Man and Superman* (Act III):

> *Mendoza:* I am a brigand: I live by robbing the rich.
> *Tanner:* I am a gentleman: I live by robbing the poor. Shake hands.

All these examples remind us that the satiric character can possess only a limited independence. More than most fictional characters he is the creature of his maker. No matter what he is in himself, he always remains the creature of his master's satiric intention. The satiric position is defined early in a work and the character serves to illustrate it. He does not become; he is. He does not develop, or if he does, he may, as happens to some extent with Joseph Andrews, outgrow his creator's original purpose. His action will be basically repetitive; his interest will lie in incidental versatility, in the way in which the author plays the satiric variations on his theme. If he is an evil or unpleasant character, the author can also exploit the reader's expectations of retribution. This occurs with Bounderby and the characters in *The Alchemist*. We need to recognize, however, that a character may be only partially satiric. Thus Mrs Elton in *Emma* is, in Forsterian terms, a 'round' character like others in the novel. There are certain aspects of her behaviour which Jane Austen wants, and wants us, to ridicule; there are others which we are called upon simply to condemn. This distinction, of course, is not clear-cut; the characterization is too complex for that. We cannot maintain a proper satiric distance as she tries so insistently and with such obvious lack of welcome to patronize Jane Fairfax, but the quality of our criticism is influenced by the satirical angles from which we have already viewed her. She comes into the novel first as Emma sees her and we are pre-pared to make allowances for Emma's bias. When the latter reflects on Mrs Elton's being the daughter of 'a Bristol – merchant, of course, he must be called', we note Emma's sense of her own social position and think that her contempt for trade may be lead-ing her to be less than fair to Mrs Elton (Ch. 22). The irony is that she could not be less than fair; Mrs Elton boasts of wealth and possessions, and these not even her own, but her sister's. In subtle ways Jane Austen reflects on her vulgarity – her familiarity in addressing Knightley, her pretence to smartness in calling him 'Mr K', and even more silly, her husband 'caro sposo'. Her whole vocabulary is liberally sprinkled with fashionable *clichés*. When enough has been said, she can be summed up in the best Jane Austen concise manner – 'self-important, presuming, familiar, ignorant and ill-bred' (Ch. 33). Mrs Elton is a well-executed mix-ture of condemnation, by which Jane Austen says what she means, and satire, by which she means something other than what she often says.

WORDS, SYNTAX, VERSE AND IMAGERY

Parody often depends exclusively on words and we may there-fore fitly begin this section with a paragraph or two about it. Parody is essentially mimicry. In this sense it resembles mock-epic, except that it is less formal and more verbal. Thus Shakespeare uses Pistol with his:

> Shall pack-horses
> And hollow pamper'd jades of Asia
> Which cannot go but thirty mile a day
> Compare with Caesars and with Cannibals?
> (2 Henry IV, II. iv. 160–3)

to maltreat the bombastic manner of Marlowe's:

> Holla, ye pampered jades of Asia!
> What! can ye draw but twenty miles a day?
> (Tamburlaine, Part II, IV. iv. 1–2)

But Shakespeare in his turn found his parodist in Max Beerbohm's 'Savonarola', in Act II of which we have the following reminiscence of the chop-logic, the pseudo-learning, the punning and the gay inconsequent lyrics of the Shakespearean fool:

> For, marry, if the cobbler stuck to his last, then were his latest his last *in rebus ambulantibus*. Argal, I stick at nothing but cobble-stones which, by the same token, are stuck to the road by men's fingers ...

> When pears hang green on the garden wall
>> With a nid, and a nod, and a niddy-niddy-o
> Then prank you, lads and lasses all
>> With a yea and a nay and a niddy-o.

Beerbohm's versatility extended to the imitation of his contemporaries. Thus the diabolism of 'Nocturne':

> Round and round the shutter'd Square
> I stroll'd with the Devil's arm in mine,
> No sound but the scrape of his hoofs was there
> And the ring of his laughter and mine.
> We had drunk black wine.

Lord David Cecil succinctly defined successful parody when he said of these pieces: 'So near to the real thing, Soames's poems are

just more absurd than the typical Yellow Book poem of the time.'
(Beerbohm, *Seven Men and Two Others*, Oxford (World's
Classics), London, 1966, p. xi.) There it is – all-but-identical but
also subtly exaggerated. It may be the exact verbal and syntactical
form but applied to a ridiculous subject, or it may be the same
subject with the slightest verbal or syntactical alteration. In the
work of the contemporary playwright Harold Pinter there is
hardly even the slight change. He often achieves his effect simply
by making his audience aware of everyday colloquial exchanges
with all their hesitation, incompleteness, incoherence and inanity.

The minute change of reference is crucial in satire. It may be a
well-known allusion employed in an unconventional way, as when
Eliot makes the telling contrast between the Elizabethan Thames
of Spenser's *Prothalamion* and the river of today, sordid both
actually and in its associations:

> The nymphs are departed.
> Sweet Thames, run softly till I end my song.
> The river bears no empty bottles, sandwich papers,
> Silk handkerchiefs, cardboard boxes, cigarette ends
> Or other testimony of summer nights. The nymphs are departed.
> And their friends, the loitering heirs of city directors.
>
> > *(The Waste Land*, 175–80)

There are whole passages of this poem which it is possible to
consider as a patchwork quilt of satire by allusion. These lines also
illustrate the use of a whole list of references to build up a criticism.
We have it again in Pope's reference to Sporus, spitting himself
abroad

> In Puns, or Politicks, or Tales, or Lies,
> Or Spite, or Smut, or Rymes, or Blasphemies,
>
> > *(Epistle to Dr Arbuthnot*, 321–2)

and in the paraphernalia of Belinda's dressing-table with its

> Puffs, Powders, Patches, Bibles, Billet-doux.
>
> > *(The Rape of the Lock.* I 138)

In this last example there is the added force of inverted anticlimax in 'Bibles'. The whole of Belinda's world is trivial, but suddenly its triviality is brought into starker focus by the reference to something really important. Gray provides an interesting example of a mock-climax followed by an anticlimax in the 'Ode on the Death of a Favourite Cat'. The cat's attempt to catch the goldfish is described in terms of hyperbole. The whole affair is ludicrously inflated:

> The hapless nymph with wonder saw.

The inflation of this is evident when the next line reads:

> A whisker first, and then a claw.

The poet brings the stanza to its moralizing climax, a mock-climax:

> What female heart can gold despise?

only to bring this exaltation crashing down with the resoundingly prosaic last line of anticlimax:

> What Cat's averse to fish?

Satiric effect by reduction in the level of discourse, as here, can also be achieved by the insertion of colloquialism. This is illustrated in the speech of Sir Plume in *The Rape of the Lock* (quoted above, p. 44), though there it also serves the function of parody. A particularly brilliant example of the use of the colloquial is to be found in Dryden's portrait of Corah (Titus Oates), reflecting on the latter's claim to a doctorate of divinity from the University of Salamanca:

> The spirit caught him up, the Lord knows where;
> And gave him his rabbinical degree,
> Unknown to foreign university,
>
> (*Absalom and Achitophel*, 657–9)

where 'the Lord knows where' is appropriate to the meanness which Dryden finds in Oates, is further suggestive of the fact that

Oates's fertile imagination bears no relationship to the truth, and hints at the Puritan emphasis on divine guidance in even the least affairs of life. There is also a suggestion of alcoholic fantasy in the pun on 'spirit'. Pope has a more subtle pun based on addiction to drink in:

> Bentley late tempestuous wont to sport
> In troubled waters, but now sleeps in Port.
>
> (*The Dunciad* IV. 201–2)

with the added refinement of a note by his Dr Scriblerus, whose mock-scholarly detail adds still further to the satire of the scholar Bentley. The pun is a form of innuendo, but its two incongruous meanings are usually more readily, even obviously, recognizable than those of innuendo proper. The latter depends, in fact, for its effect on the slight delay in realizing that a second meaning underlies the first and obvious meaning. Thus the last phrase in Pope's reference

> To happy Convents, bosom'd deep in vines,
> Where slumber Abbots, purple as their wines,
>
> (*The Dunciad* IV. 301–2)

is apparently only descriptive, but we soon realize that it is also critical. The abbots' complexion is not unrelated to their bibulousness. Likewise, Belinda's protest

> 'Oh hadst thou, Cruel! been content to seize
> Hairs less in sight, or any Hairs but these!'
>
> (*The Rape of the Lock* IV. 175–6)

that looks simply like the climax of her distress, suddenly suggests new implications. What other hairs? The sexual reference becomes apparent, and the innuendo discloses an attitude that exalts reputation (the distress at an incident known to everybody) above honour.

There are similar suggestions in the device of the doubtful antecedent in:

> On her white Breast a sparkling *Cross* she wore,
> Which *Jews* might kiss, and Infidels adore.
>
> (Ibid., II., 7–8)

Does 'which' refer to 'Cross' or 'breast'? And when we consider the question, does it matter? If they kiss the cross, they are near enough to the breast. We may note also the nice ambiguity in 'might' – is it in the sense of 'would be driven to' – or is it 'would be allowed to'? In the second line here the second example works by a simple reinforcement. Such second examples often work by contrast. We have already noticed the effect of zeugma in the line:

> Or stain her Honour, or her new Brocade.
>
> (Ibid., II., 107)

Another instance occurs in the couplet:

> Not louder Shrieks to pitying Heaven are cast,
> When Husbands or when Lap-dogs breathe their last.
>
> (Ibid., III., 157–8)

Here we have in this example of hyperbole something also of the effect of negation. Much of *The Rape of the Lock*, the poem being high burlesque, is exaggeration or hyperbole. In the second line there is an implicit antithesis, again as so often in this poem, working in inverted fashion. The lapdogs do better than the husbands.

Devices of the kind referred to in the previous paragraph depend extensively on syntactical arrangements within the overall sentence structure – the reference of a relative pronoun, the relationship of two objects, the placing of the negative, for instance. A host of other devices rest on a similar basis, and especially on the balance or relationship of parts. This is illustrated by antithesis in Wilde's

> All women become like their mothers. That is their tragedy. No man does. That's his.
>
> (*The Importance of Being Earnest*, Act I)

inversion in Pope's

> Proud as *Apollo* on his forkèd hill
> Sat full-blown *Bufo*, puffed by every quill,
>> (*Epistle to Dr Arbuthnot*, 231–2)

where the grandeur of the first line is deflated by the reality of the second; chiasmus in the same author's

> A Fop their Passion, but their Prize a Sot,
>> (*Epistles to Several Persons* II. 247)

where contrast in the second half is heightened by inversion; parallelism (with stress on implicit contrasts) in:

> Where, in nice balance, truth with gold she weighs,
> And solid pudding against empty praise.
>> (*The Dunciad* I. 53–4)

Finally, there is repetition, sometimes achieving its effects by simple insistence as in the phrase 'A man' in Dickens's description of Bounderby, sometimes by the reiteration of a word with a slight alteration of meaning as in:

> Secure his person to secure your cause:
> They who possess the prince possess the laws.
>> (*Absalom and Achitophel*, 475–6)

The second of these lines exemplifies another satiric device, the use of 'sententiae' or concise generalizing statements. They particularly suit moral satire of the kind typified by Johnson's *Vanity of Human Wishes*:

> How rarely reason guides the stubborn choice ...
> Life protracted, is protracted woe ...,

but they also appear with effect as points of summary in more personal satire. Thus

> Great wits are sure to madness near allied,
> And thin partitions do their bounds divide.
>> (*Absalom and Achitophel*, 163–4)

has a general truth and an effective particular application in the middle of Dryden's portrait of Achitophel. The same passage also illustrates the satiric use of rhetorical question, as Dryden goes on:

> Else why should he, with wealth and honour blest,
> Refuse his age the needful hours of rest?
>
> (Ibid., 165–6)

but an even better example is:

> But who can know
> How far the devil and Jebusites may go?
>
> (Ibid., 132–3)

The treatment of Achitophel ends with exclamation in the form of lament:

> Oh! had he been content to serve the crown.
> With virtues only proper to the gown.
>
> (Ibid., 192–3)

whilst another form of exclamation much favoured by satirists is that of apostrophe. Thus Pope ironically has the goddess Dulness encourage one of her devotees:

> Flow, Welsted, flow! like thine inspirer, Beer,
>
> (*The Dunciad* III. 169)

and in tones of outrage Byron bursts forth of Wordsworth:

> 'Pedlars', and 'Boats', and 'Waggons!' Oh! ye shades
> Of Pope and Dryden, are we come to this ...
> The 'little boatman' and his *Peter Bell*
> Can sneer at him who drew 'Achitophel'!
>
> (*Don Juan*, Canto III, stanza 100)

These examples of word- and sentence-usage have been drawn almost exclusively from verse, and even from verse in heroic couplets. The reason for this is that this form, at any rate as it was developed and perfected by Pope and Dryden, with its emphasis on economy, precision and conciseness, provides many of the best brief examples. There was a double and contradictory set of influences at work on the satiric measure of the sixteenth and seventeenth centuries. Horace had spoken of his own easy-going satiric verse as being 'sermoni propiora' or, in Dryden's phrase, 'nearest prose' (*Religio Laici*, 454), whilst Juvenal's hexameters had been much more forceful, at times even epigrammatic. English satire began, however, with belief in a rough measure. This may have owed something to Skelton, whose doggerel measures are in the tradition of medieval goliardic verses. He himself described it, even as he was exemplifying it, in *Colin Clout*:

> For though my rhyme be ragged,
> Tattered and jagged,
> Rudely rain-beaten,
> Rusty and moth-eaten,
> If ye take well therewith,
> It hath in it some pith.

Certainly in Donne the heroic couplet of a later day is hard to recognize:

> Seek true religion. O, where? Mirreus,
> Thinking her unhoused here, and fled from us,
> Seeks her at Rome; there, because he doth know
> That she was there a thousand years ago.
>
> (Satire III. 43–6)

There is a process of gradual polishing of the couplet through such writers as Cleveland, Marvell and Oldham until one reaches Dryden, and he, we must remember, did not attain that ideal of correctness which Pope set himself and the shortcomings in regard to which he illustrated with such point and wit in the *Essay on Criticism* (II. 344–83). Pope there writes that

> True Ease in Writing comes from Art, not Chance,

and in this respect the heroic couplet conveys the sense of being a highly wrought, sophisticated and artificial form.

It could suggest a variety of attitudes – stupidity as in the lines on Welsted quoted above or silliness as in the near-jingling and feminine rhymes of Dryden on Zimri:

> Then all for women, painting, rhyming, drinking
> Besides ten thousand freaks that died in thinking,
>
> (*Absalom and Achitophel*, 551–2)

but there were those who preferred freer and less elevated forms. Swift showed how the octosyllabic couplet has a freedom that accommodated well with a colloquial idiom, as in 'A Satirical Elegy on the Death of a Late Famous General [Marlborough]':

> His Grace! Impossible! what, dead!
> Of old age too, and in his bed!
>
> (1–2)

at the same time revealing the measure's versatility as he changed to a moralizing tone:

> Come hither, all ye empty things,
> Ye bubbles raised by breath of kings.
>
> (25–6)

Yet another free form, at any rate as the satirist used it, is Byron's *ottava rima* in *Don Juan* with the added attraction of its outrageous rhymes:

> Some persons say that Dante meant theology
> By Beatrice, and not a mistress – I,
> Although my opinion may require apology,
> Deem this a commentator's phantasy.
>
> (Canto III. 81–4)

Various in its subjects and its modes, so too is satire in its forms. Measures long, short, stanzaic, free, all come aptly to its hand, and likewise with prose. One demand alone it makes, that not a phrase be wasted, that every word carry its full weight of meaning.

The imagery of satire is likewise various. It is always denigratory. When it seems otherwise, it will only seem; it will probably be meant to be read in either distorted or inverted mode. Because it is denigratory, it will often take for comparison the trivial, or worse, the ugly and repulsive. With that deliberate superficiality which is one of his weapons, Byron in *The Vision of Judgment* speaks of all those against George III who were

> Ready to swear against the good king's reign,
> Bitter as clubs in cards are against spades,

> (Stanza 60)

whilst in the comparison quoted above Pope goes on to describe the beer to which he likened Welsted as

> Tho' stale, not ripe; tho' thin, yet never clear.
> (*The Dunciad* III. 170)

There is here a partial (and distorted) echo of Denham's lines about the Thames in *Cooper's Hill*, so that this becomes a double-comparison. My point, however, is to indicate the level, the prosaic and ordinary, even the debased, that Pope is employing for Welsted. Going further to the ugly and repulsive, one notes the popularity of insect-imagery, the variety of effect of which can be estimated from a parallel, say, of Dryden's locust image (see above, p. 40), Swift's reference to the 'race of little odious vermin' (see above, p. 37) and Pope's comparison of Sporus, 'this Bug with gilded wings', in a portrait that goes on to emphasize the poet's antipathy with an accumulation of images including the fawning spaniel, 'familiar Toad' and 'Eve's tempter ... A Cherub's face, a Reptile all the rest' (*Epistle to Dr Arbuthnot*, 309–33). In Swift the parallels go even further than this to repugnant sexual and excretory references.

4
Tones

Melville Clark's list is sufficiently comprehensive – 'wit, ridicule, irony, sarcasm, cynicism, the sardonic and invective'. All these hurt, because satire aims to hurt, but, as with the bull-fighter, so with the satirist, his competence lies not in his ability to do his job but rather in the skill he deploys in doing it. If we regard the list above as a series of weapons, wit, as it is so often said to be, is the rapier and invective is Churchill's 'flail', or perhaps more accurately the bludgeon. To quote Dryden, 'a man may be capable, as Jack Ketch's wife said of his servant, of a plain piece of work, a bare hanging; but to make a malefactor die sweetly was only belonging to her husband' (*Discourse Concerning Satire*).

Wit wounds with a neat and unexpected stroke. Its exponent needs, mentally, all the grace, speed and dexterity of the fencer. The reader is surprised, comically shocked, by the unexpected collocation of ideas; yet though unexpected, he recognizes in them a certain truth or at any rate sufficient truth for the wit to be acceptable. Thus Tacitus's remark about Galba – 'capax imperii nisi imperasset' (a likely ruler had he never ruled) – neatly summarizes both that emperor's promise and his failure. The epigram with its structural brevity is a favoured vehicle of wit. Thus of another ruler Rochester wrote:

> Here lies our Sovereign Lord the King,
> Whose word no man relies on,
> Who never said a foolish thing
> Nor ever did a wise one.

('Epitaph on Charles II')

In two lines Blake manages to turn a situation both on his victim and himself:

> A petty Sneaking Knave I knew;
> Oh Mr Cr[omek], how do ye do?

Dryden follows the remark about Jack Ketch with a reference to his own characterization of Zimri: ''Tis not bloody, but 'tis ridiculous enough.' Like wit, ridicule should be good-tempered. Whatever it has of derision about it should be kept in control and counter-balanced by teasing raillery. He analyses his treatment of Zimri thus: 'I avoided the mention of great crimes, and applied myself to the representing of blind sides, and little extravagancies.' Ridicule, as the etymology of the word indicates, is essentially laughing satire. This places certain subjects and attitudes outside its scope. 'What could exceed the absurdity of an author, who should write the comedy of Nero, with the merry incident of ripping his mother's belly?' (Fielding, Preface to *Joseph Andrews*). In our own age with its emulation of that of Nero we have had such comedy, but it is ironic 'black comedy', ridicule gone sour. Pure ridicule must confine itself to lighter things. Fielding went on to claim: 'The only source of the true Ridiculous (as it appears to me) is affectation ... Now, affectation proceeds from one of these two causes, vanity or hypocrisy.' And the best way to cure these is not to get into a passion about them but simply to make the victim look silly and thus regain the norm which has been distorted.

By contrast, irony uses distortion as its weapon, total distortion in the form of inversion. It is not simply inversion, either. It includes in its effect implication, insinuation and omission. It requires a select and responsive audience to recognize its peculiar direction of meaning. Otherwise, as happened to Swift with *The Modest Proposal*, the readers may think that the distortion is the work of a lunatic, a man whose own values have been disturbed. Beneath its surface of detachment irony conceals a passion of the deepest involvement. Because it is so involved, its effects are often best obtained over the broad scope of a whole work, such as, for instance, *A Modest Proposal* or Fielding's *Jonathan Wild*, but irony may also contribute to something that is not, over all, ironic. Thus the lines

> 'It grieves me much' (replied the Peer again)
> 'Who speaks so well should ever speak in vain.'
>
> (*The Rape of the Lock* IV. 131–2)

in response to the incoherent splutterings of Sir Plume are manifestly anything but the truth. Likewise, when Swift writes: 'Last week I saw a woman flayed, and you will hardly believe how much it altered her person for the worse,' these words, though set in the pervasively ironic 'Digression Concerning Madness' (*A Tale of a Tub*, Section IX), give to the irony a deeper incidental intensity. This is, in fact, an example of irony by understatement, the appearance of representing something as much less serious than it really is. As with Gulliver in the visit to Brobdingnag and the author of *A Modest Proposal* Swift achieves his irony in part by the *persona* of an excessively naïve or imperceptive narrator.

Sarcasm is irony without the mystery and the refinement. It is essentially incidental and verbal. It is also cruder than irony, a much blunter instrument. It is lacking in generosity. It has been called, not without justice, the lowest form of wit. Verbal irony, especially if it is only merely incidental sarcasm, may well not be recognized in the written form. It does better in a dramatic context, as, for example, when we know the difference between the reality and Falstaff's pretence about the Gadshill ambush. Though he boasts of his valour we know that he and his comrades were put to flight almost without a struggle. In these circumstances we can appreciate Hal's sarcasm when he says: 'Pray God you have not murd'red some of them' (*1 Henry IV*, II. iv. 182–3). When we know the true state of things, sarcasm can be telling. Thus Junius, writing of the Duke of Grafton's rejection of statesmen like Chatham, Rockingham and Wilkes for a group of men all notorious for qualities exactly opposite to those which he (Junius) ascribes to them, confesses that the rejected were not

> ill exchanged for the youthful, vigorous virtue of the Duke of Bedford; – the firmness of General Conway, the awkward integrity of Mr Rigby, and the spotless morality of Lord Sandwich.
>
> (Letter 14 – 22 June 1769, *Letters of Junius*,
> ed. C. W. Everett, London, 1927, p. 67)

Cynicism and the sardonic are closely related. Both of them issue from a deep sense of disillusion, and the two often occur in close relationship. Byron is on the frontier of the two when he writes:

> And if I laugh at any mortal thing,
> 'Tis that I may not weep.
>
> (*Don Juan*, Canto IV, stanza 4)

The cynic's criticisms are made against the background of hollow laughter; the sardonic comment is too pessimistic to accept even hollow laughter. The speaker may laugh, but his will be a lonely and embittered delight. Byron's own cynicism takes the form of flippancy, of a refusal to be serious:

> Let us have wine and women, mirth and laughter,
> Sermons and soda water the day after.
>
> Man being reasonable, must get drunk;
> The best of life is but intoxication:
> Glory, the grape, love, gold, in these are sunk
> The hopes of all men, and of every nation.
>
> (Ibid., Canto II, stanzas 178–9)

Amid the social protest of *The Village* Crabbe introduces a note of cynicism, darker than Byron's. Like Swift, but without his intensity, Crabbe is fascinated by unpleasant actuality:

F

> By such examples taught, I paint the cot,
> As Truth will paint it, and as bards will not.
>
> (I. 53–4)

He then puts bards and Truth together:

> Where are the swains, who, daily labour done,
> With rural games played down the setting sun ...
> Where now are these? – Beneath yon cliff they stand,
> To show the freighted pinnace where to land ...
>
> (Ibid., 93–4, 101–2)

The idealistic fantasy – pastoral innocence; the cynical reality –
lawless smuggling.

The sardonic would rather weep than laugh. Thus when in a
single line Pope turns from his general portrait to a precise
identification, he uses just these words as the mood changes and
the reader recognizes with sorrow the person who has seemed so
much other than Pope says he is:

> Who but must laugh, if such a man there be?
> Who would not weep, if *Atticus* were he?
>
> (*Epistle to Dr Arbuthnot*, 213–14)

As Melville Clark puts it, 'the laughter of the cynic is edged with
contempt, but sardonic laughter is blunted with chagrin and
mortification' (op. cit., p. 49). But the sardonic is on the edge of
weeping because it is on the edge of uncontrollable anger. That is
why its laugh is so bitter. Swift has expressed this aspect of the
sardonic position:

> Like the ever-laughing Sage
> In a Jest I spend my Rage
> (Tho' it must be understood
> I would hang them if I cou'd:)
>
> ('Epistle to A Lady', 171–4)

The anger that the sardonic manages to keep under control
bursts forth in invective. This extreme of the satiric spectrum

makes a direct and unremitting attack on its object. It may seek to act as the mouthpiece of public indignation. Thus Junius of the Duke of Grafton begins sarcastically: 'Come forward, thou virtuous minister, and tell the world by what interest Mr Hine has been recommended to so extraordinary a mark of his Majesty's favour' and goes on relentlessly:

> Do you dare to prosecute such a creature as Vaughan, while you are basely setting up the Royal Patronage to auction? Do you dare to complain of an attack upon your own honour, while you are selling the favours of the crown, to raise a fund for corrupting the morals of the people? And do you think it possible that such enormities should escape without impeachment? It is indeed highly your interest to maintain the present house of commons. Having sold the nation to you in gross, they will undoubtedly protect you in the detail; for while they patronize your crimes, they feel for their own.
>
> (Letter 33 – 29 Nov. 1769, *Letters of Junius*,
> ed. C. W. Everett, 1927, p. 131)

Such invective often descends to the level of personal lampoon, as with Junius's repeated reference to Grafton's illegitimate descent from, and comparable sexual propensities to those of, Charles II. It may even fall to abuse and the calling of names. In late medieval Scotland the 'flyting' or war of words in abusive fashion was a recognized literary mode. One of the best examples is Dunbar's 'The Flyting of Dunbar and Kennedy'. It includes colourful name-calling, candid remarks on physical appearance and caustic reflection on character:

> Mauch muttoun, byt buttoun, peilit gluttoun, air to Hilhous;
>   Rank beggar, ostir dregar, foule fleggar in the flet;
> Chittirlilling, ruch rilling, lik schilling in the milhous;
>   Baird rehator, theif of natour, fals tratour, feyindis gett; . . .
>   Herretyk, lunatyk, purspyk, carlingis pet,
> Rottin crok, dirtin dok, cry cok, or I sall quell the.

(Maggotty old sheep, button-biter, hairless glutton, Hillhouse's heir;
   Evil-smelling beggar, greedy scavenger, dirty scarecrow in the
    shadows;
Scrap of pig's guts, rough-shod lout, mill-house scrounger;
   Poets' foe, natural-born thief, false traitor, Satan's brat; ...
   Heretic, lunatic, cut-purse, old woman's darling,
Rotten old ewe, filthy arse, give up the game before I lay you out
   cold!)[1]

This may well be part of what was just a contest (contrast, for example, Dunbar's tribute to Kennedy in *The Lament for the Makaris*), but even if it be feigned, it serves to illustrate my point. We have got as far from true wit as it is possible to go. 'How easy is it to call rogue and villain, and that wittily! But how hard to make a man appear a fool, a blockhead, or a knave, without using any of these opprobrious terms!' (Dryden, *Discourse Concerning Satire*).

[1] I am indebted for this rendering to my friend, Dr A. M. Kinghorn, Reader in English in the University of the West Indies.

5
Conclusion – The Satirist and the Reader

Satire always has a victim, it always criticizes. Why does the satirist act in this way? His first task is to convince his audience of the worth – even more, of the necessity – of what he is doing. He must mean, or at any rate convince his readers that he means, what he says. The unconvinced reader reacts as Quiller-Couch did when he wrote:

> Few will deny Juvenal's force: yet after all as we open a volume entitled *Sixteen Satires of Juvenal*, what are we promised but this – 'Go to! I Decimus Junius Juvenalis, propose to lose my temper on sixteen several occasions'?
>
> (*Studies in Literature*, First Series, 1937 edn., p. 49)

What Quiller-Couch is saying is that Juvenal is too engaged. He, the reader, is not interested either in bad temper or the simulation of it. The author must either avoid it or show very strong reason indeed for indulging it.

One way of doing the latter is to allege the magnitude of the need for satire and the satirist's role as a public benefactor. Thus Swift felt that things were so bad that he could write: 'The chief end I propose to my self in all my labours is to vex the world rather than divert it.' He also with his customary candour saw that there were

> two ends that Men propose in writing Satyr, one of them less noble than the other, as regarding nothing further than the private Satis-faction, and Pleasure of the Writer ... The other is a publick Spirit, prompting men of genius, to mend the world as far as they are able.
>
> (*The Intelligencer*, Vol. III (1728),
> *Prose Works*, Vol. XII, p. 34)

In his mischievous private role the satirist must carry his reader by the virtuosity of his art, because he cannot rely on mere malice. He cannot even rely on a private dispute, however righteous he may think his own cause: 'It is great vanity to think anyone will attend to a thing, because it is your quarrel' (Steele, *Tatler*, No. 242). Indeed, in this essay Steele argues the need for good nature as an 'essential quality in a satirist', because 'the ordinary subjects for satire are such as incite the greatest indignation in the best tempers'. Men of such make are also capable of the necessary detachment: 'There is a certain impartiality necessary to make what a man says bear any weight with those he speaks to.' The satirist may be abnormally sensitive, disillusioned, alienated, prejudiced, but, to have the best hope of success, he must appear detached, well-balanced, judicious and, did but the world allow it, capable of being better-natured than he seems.

His aim is to move his readers to criticize and condemn and he will seek to do so by moving them to various emotions ranging from laughter through ridicule, contempt and anger to hate. The feelings evoked will depend on the seriousness of the faults attacked as well as on the stance which the author himself adopts, the view he takes of the gap between the ideal and the reality. It is superfluous to quote examples; they abound in the preceding pages. Roughly, the feelings mentioned above parallel that series of tones running from light wit to savage irony.

The reader must be persuaded, and the difficulty in doing this is not merely a matter of overcoming an unwillingness to criticize. When he is prepared to do this, what happens then? Where does he stand? He realizes that in criticizing, he is taking pleasure at another's discomfort, but he is also tacitly assuming his own superiority or congratulating himself on his own escape. Such reactions are easier, the nearer we are to the circumstances in question. Pope's readers could enjoy his victims' discomforts, because they might know the victims and feel that they deserved their fate. For us that degree of engagement is impossible, and yet living satire must somehow be able to make us re-live the original experience. It does so, as the preceding pages have tried to show, in one or both of two ways – by convincing us that the underlying attitudes have a permanent significance transcending the ephemeral circumstances or by the sheer artistry in the execution of the satire. To put it in the words which that great satirist Horace felt summed up the function of all literature, by instruction and delight.

Bibliography

ALDEN, R. M., *The Rise of Formal Verse Satire in England under Classical Influence*, Philadelphia, 1899; reprinted Hamden, Conn., 1961.

Quite full consideration of Elizabethan satirists in terms of the book's title.

BOULTON, J. T. and KINSLEY, J. (edd.), *English Satiric Poetry, Dryden to Byron*, London, 1966.

Selections with thoughtful introduction.

CLARK, A. M., *Studies in Literary Modes*, Edinburgh, 1946.

Chapter 2 has reflections on satire.

ELLIOTT, R. C., *The Power of Satire: Magic, Ritual, Art*, Princeton, 1960.

Wide-ranging, going back to anthropological and primitive sources.

FRYE, N., *The Anatomy of Criticism*, Princeton, N.J., 1957.

Section on 'The Mythos of Winter: Irony and Satire'.

HIGHET, G., *The Anatomy of Satire*, Princeton, 1962.

Stimulating criticism covering several European literatures. The reader should also consult his lively *Juvenal the Satirist*.

HODGART, M., *Satire*, London, 1969.

Excellent range of reference, perceptive comment and brilliant pictorial examples.

HOPKINS, K., *Portraits in Satire*, London, 1958.

On the lesser eighteenth-century satirists.

JACK, I., *Augustan Satire, 1660–1750*, Oxford, 1952.

Mainly on Dryden and Pope but also has chapters on Butler and Dr Johnson. Discriminates between the various forms of Augustan satire.

KERNAN, A., *The Cankered Muse: Satire of the English Renaissance*, New Haven, 1959.

Satirist versus fools, with special emphasis on drama.

KERNAN, A., *The Plot of Satire*, New Haven, 1965.

Claims that satire dramatizes (and unifies) the two components, art and morality.

LEYBURN, E. D., *Satiric Allegory: Mirror of Man*, New Haven, 1956.

Deals with the various forms considered under Satiric Allegories (pp. 28–40 above).

MACDONALD, D., *Parodies: an Anthology from Chaucer to Beerbohm – and after*, New York, 1960.

PAULSON, R., *The Fictions of Satire*, Baltimore, 1967.

'If satire originates as rhetoric, or attack, it only matters – or survives as literature – as mimesis, exploration, and analysis' (pp. 7–8). Satire as 'fictional construct'.

Satire and the Novel in Eighteenth-Century England, New Haven, 1967.

Extends the method of the previous book to the novel. Especially good on Smollett.

PETER, J., *Complaint and Satire in Early English Literature*, Oxford, 1956.

Traces complaint and satire through medieval sermon to Marston and Tourneur.

SMEATON, O., *English Satires*, London, 1899.

Selection with introduction.

SUTHERLAND, J., *English Satire*, Cambridge, 1958.

Clark Lectures at Cambridge. Broad survey with shrewd critical remarks.

THOMSON, J. A. K., *Classical Influences on English Poetry*, London, 1951.

Chapter 10 on satire. Better on Latin than on English writers, but interesting consideration.

WALKER, H., *English Satire and Satirists*, London, 1925.

Detailed survey of both the great and the small among English satirists.

WOLFE, H., *Notes on English Verse Satire*, London, 1929.

Idiosyncratic and provocative.

WORCESTER, D., *The Art of Satire*, Cambridge, Mass., 1940; reprinted New York, 1960.

Looks at such subjects as invective, epigram, burlesque, comic and tragic irony.

NOTE: The reader should also consult critical works on individual authors. The British Council's *Writers and Their Work* series of essays includes the major English satirists and each volume has a fairly extensive annotated bibliography.

Index

Index